Lynne Carter has run an astrology practice, having gained her certificate with the Faculty of Astrological Studies in 2002. She continued her studies and gained her Diploma in 2008, based on the work *Christian Astrology* by William Lilly.

She has worked with modern and medieval techniques, producing personalised charts for each of her clients. She has regularly appeared at Mind, Body, and Soul exhibitions in London and the Home Counties, conducted workshops with astrology groups, as well as teaching beginners.

Since her arrival in Scotland, she has presented radio broadcasts for Dunoon Community Radio and appearing at holistic events in Glasgow.

In memory of
Maureen Ross (1926–2008)
Eric Ross (1908–1978)
Verna Ross (1957–2009)
Janet Evans (1939–1997)

Lynne Carter

Draw Back the Curtain

For Those Who Didn't Know
Astrology Was There

Austin Macauley Publishers
LONDON · CAMBRIDGE · NEW YORK · SHARJAH

Copyright © Lynne Carter 2025

The right of Lynne Carter to be identified as author of this work has been asserted by the author in accordance with sections 77 and 78 of the Copyright, Designs and Patents Act 1988.

All rights reserved. No part of this publication may be reproduced, stored in a retrieval system, or transmitted in any form or by any means, electronic, mechanical, photocopying, recording, or otherwise, without the prior permission of the publishers.

Any person who commits any unauthorised act in relation to this publication may be liable to criminal prosecution and civil claims for damages.

The story, experiences, and words are the author's alone.

A CIP catalogue record for this title is available from the British Library.

ISBN 9781037110740 (Paperback)
ISBN 9781037110757 (ePub e-book)

www.austinmacauley.com

First Published 2025
Austin Macauley Publishers Ltd®
1 Canada Square
Canary Wharf
London
E14 5AA

Table of Contents

Part 1   **13**

   Chapter 1: The Gift   *15*

   Chapter 2: Your First Birthday Present   *19*

Part 2   **39**

   Chapter 3: The Ages   *41*

   Chapter 4: What Makes You Think We Can Tell You   *47*

   Chapter 5: The Planets   *56*

   Chapter 6: The Signs   *81*

   Chapter 7: Planetary Conditions   *96*

   Chapter 8: The Houses   *100*

   Chapter 9: The Nodes of the Moon   *113*

Part 3   **117**

   Chapter 10: An Astrological Act of Remembrance   *119*

   Chapter 11: To Close   *129*

Bibliography   **130**

Draw Back the Curtain

This book is designed for those who have no knowledge of astrology. It is not designed for professional astrologers or students, owing to its simplicity in the wording. However, Chapter 2 may be of benefit to students as to the location of common astrological terms. This was raised when I was a student.

Chapter 1 explains what a chart is and is doing.

Chapters 3–7 deal with the fundamental meanings of the signs, planets, houses and what happens at certain ages.

Chapter 9 deals with something we have to achieve, and this will always take us out of our comfort zone.

Chapter 10 looks into the astrology surrounding the sinking of the Titanic, rewritten since the finding of new evidence. Charts have been provided to back up all information.

A list of signs and planets is at the front of the book, but I have also included them in the script for ease.

Lynne Carter
DT Astrol

Signs of the Zodiac

Aries	♈
Taurus	♉
Gemini	♊
Cancer	♋
Leo	♌
Virgo	♍
Libra	♎
Scorpio	♏
Sagittarius	♐
Capricorn	♑
Aquarius	♒
Pisces	♓
The Planets	
Sun	☉

Moon	☽
Mercury	☿
Venus	♀
Mars	♂
Jupiter	♃
Saturn	♄
Uranus	⛢
Neptune	♆
Pluto	♇

Part 1

*To everything there is a season
and a time to every purpose under heaven.*

Chapter 1
The Gift

If someone were to say to you, 'We are going on a long journey', the first thing that would cross your mind is: *How are we going to get there?* No doubt there would be time spent looking at maps and planning a route, and if you are into modern technology, a sat-nav is a must. This is accepted behaviour—thought and planning are put to good use to make sure there are no mishaps along the way.

Having said that, how many people start on the longest journey of all—the journey of life—without realising they have a map, much less use it? This map has a second function: it is also a clock—our personal timing device. This map and clock follow you everywhere, working quietly in the background, causing all the major events in your life to which you have often said:

'Why me?'

'Why has this happened now?'

'I just happened to be in the right place at the right time.'

None of this is coincidental. Your mystery map and clock just happen to be your birth chart—your first birthday present. The gift that was given to you at the moment you were born, and the gift that will stay with you throughout your life, unravelling its secrets as time goes on.

All the good things in life that you experience—your talents, gifts, enjoyment and relationships—are all hidden in this map. This also goes for all the upsets, losses and changes that cause heartache and problems. The clock is the timing device that sets these changes in motion. It is activated by all the planets moving in the heavens and coming into contact with the planets in your natal chart, setting events in motion.

As a practicing astrologer, I have come across many incidents in people's lives that have caused illness through endless worry, or an utter sense of loss through incidents that have occurred to which they have had no control over and through no fault of their own. These changes are meant for a reason.

Some people have an inherent fear or disbelief that their chart is being activated and can hold some answers. There is a misconception that a chart removes the freedom of choice. It doesn't.

The idea of this book is not to make you into budding astrologers, but to draw your attention to the fact that this subject can help when all else fails. Whatever is going on will always be found by the planets moving around your chart.

Some people may find it hard to accept: the chart you have, you chose before your birth. Your soul incarnated at the time that it did to take on the experiences laid out by the chart. Some reading this may think it is ridiculous, when some lives are filled with grief, loss, violence, imprisonment, illness, physical or mental handicap. But all these experiences are for the development of the soul.

I would like to draw your attention to the Christmas carol 'Once in Royal David's City'. In the third verse, one line says: 'Tears and smiles like us he knew.' These tears and smiles couldn't be experienced unless in physical form on this plane. This goes for all of us—all the experiences we go through have to be dealt with here on Earth.

Another fact to take into consideration is that things never stay the same. Some people experience life-changing events which they never thought could happen to them. This can sometimes be found to be problematic, especially where relationships are concerned. In a marriage or partnership, should one person start to change or take on some form of activity or a major career change, I have often heard: 'Why can't we just stay the same as we were'.

If we did, there would be no progress or soul development. The partner experiencing the change has had their chart activated by transits, and it is time to take notice. Each of us has a job to do: a Sun sign to grow into, a wound to heal, and a path to follow. You have this lifetime to fulfil this—and it must be allowed to happen. Any obstruction can cause health problems and stress. Most people are unaware that their chart is calling for change, and they go through feelings of guilt and anxiety which are unnecessary.

There is one comment I would like to make here: Sun sign astrology is just for entertainment.

What you read in the papers can never apply to an individual, as there are so many other factors to take into account. Astrology can't be judged by the Sun alone. All the other planets have a major part to play.

Your Sun may be placed in Sagittarius, a sign that likes the outdoors, sports, and travel—especially if it's in the first house. But if the Moon be placed in a water sign, in the fourth house, your emotional needs will be tied to your home. Now we have a conflict of interest. This shows how complex we can be.

No Sun sign write-up in the tabloids can ever cover this.

Chapter 2
Your First Birthday Present

As a practicing astrologer, the one thing that has always saddened me is that some people are very afraid of this subject. What is not understood is that our world is affected by the movements of the planets. The daily movements of planets are known as *transits*—this is what is happening in space now. Astrology filters its way into every facet of our lives, working in the background while most are totally unaware it is there. Major religions have played their part in its downfall, instilling fear into the general population to the point where, in the past, astrologers and clients could pay with their lives if found out. But thankfully, astrology has made a comeback. For those who are concerned that they are going against their faith by even showing an interest, may I invite you to have a look at the Bible, 'King James' version, where there are numerous references to astrology. You may think these are open to interpretation, but two of the references need no interpretation: they are direct instructions. There are also references that only an astrologer would understand. This will be explained in this chapter, along with charts to help. To start with, we need to go back to the beginning—to the point where our solar system was born. However, you think this came about, whether by the Big Bang theory or from the Book of Genesis, you have now reached a point where the worlds of science and religion differ. There is, of course, a third possibility: the Big Bang was brought about by a deity, and everything else followed. So, if this is the case—our solar system being created in the way it is—then why can't astrology be part of that plan? During the course of time, astrology and astronomy have been separated, but going back to the Greek Philosophers, it was all one subject. Astronomy gave the geography of the heavens, and astrology gave the timing of events. This was important. Man soon learnt the importance of knowing about the Sun's orbit and eclipses. The Moon became important, as they realised how it affected the tides. Just this early knowledge gave them a chance to plan ahead.

As far as religion is concerned, the opening verses of St John's Gospel should give you an area to think about.

1. In the beginning was the Word, and the Word was God.
2. The same was in the beginning with God.
3. All things were made by Him; and without Him was not anything made that was made.

If this be the case, surely astrology was a gift given to us to help us through life.

The early Church made its thoughts felt and ruthlessly enforced its ideology on the subject. Don't be fooled—they knew the benefits of astrology. But it was not for public consumption. They kept its secrets and made themselves masters of all things spiritual. The only person who was allowed to have their chart done was the king. Astrology was used when big battles were on the horizon and, more importantly, at the birth of any prince.

The public were kept ignorant of these matters. Most couldn't read or write. The Bible was originally written in Latin, and the only access to it was in church on Sunday. Selected sections were read to the congregation. It was only when James I came to the throne that he ordered the Bible to be translated into English, so everyone could have a copy in their home. The worlds of astrology and religion are closely interlinked. I invite you to draw back the curtain and have a look.

In this section, I have included some Bible references along with relevant charts so you can see how this fits together.

Book of Isaiah, Chapter 47, Verse 13

'Thou art wearied in the multitude of thy counsels. Let now the astrologers, the stargazers, the monthly prognosticators stand up and save thee from these things that shall come upon thee.'

This is one of the direct instructions on the use of astrology in the Bible. Before the start of Christianity, astrologers were treated and respected as the clergy of their day. Here, the Lord is dissatisfied with other methods being used instead of the one provided. V11 says that **'Misfortunes will fall upon those, and they won't know where it will come from.'** This relates to astrologers being able to warn people of impending trouble. The word 'prognosticator' means forecaster.

Jeremiah, Chapter 10, Verse 2

Thus saith the Lord, **'Learn not the way of the heathen, and be not dismayed at the signs of heaven; for the heathen are dismayed at them.'**

This quote relates to other forms of forecasting—reading entrails comes to mind. People were frightened of astrological events, eclipses being the main source of fear. But again, we are being encouraged to look to the heavens for answers. Verse 3 speaks of the customs of man being vain; they were using any methods they could, except for the one that was freely given.

Ezekiel, Chapter 4, Verse 6
'I have appointed thee each day for a year.'

This extract is another entry relating to astrology. The 'day for a year' system is known as *secondary progressions*, which is a personal forecast to the individual. To start with, we need to look at a book called an *Ephemeris*, which is a daily listing of the location of the planets at any given time. I shall include a chart with this section to make it easier to understand. (Fig 1)

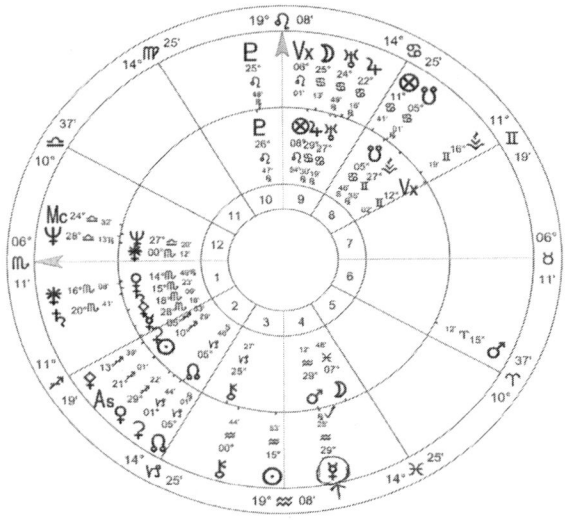

Fig 1

The planets move much slower in one of these charts. The Moon moves one degree a month. The Sun, Mercury and Venus one degree a year. So, the timing of events is only linked to you. Above is an example of a *Secondary Progressed* chart.

If you look at Mercury (☿) at the bottom of the chart's outer ring, you will see it has changed direction with an (R).

This took place when I was 62 days old, but by this system, it would be 62 years before I would feel the effect of it. So, what does it mean?

Mercury is the planet of communication, travel, and how your mind works. Placed here in the 4th house of the home, it's only now that I can sit down and write this book. Mercury is next to my natal Mars, the traditional ruler of my chart—mind and energy come together.

Acts of the Apostles

We now move to the New Testament.

Acts, Chapter 2, Verse 20

'The Sun shall be turned into darkness, and the Moon into blood.'

This, of course, is directly related to eclipses. It is well known that eclipses generated a great deal of fear among the population. What is not known is that eclipses have meaning, and should one activate your chart by coming close to planets in your natal chart, then you, the chart holder, will experience the meaning of the eclipse.

'The Sun will be turned into darkness.'

This, of course, refers to a solar eclipse, when the Sun's light is obscured as the Moon passes in front of it. A solar eclipse can be viewed as both a beginning and an ending.

The best way to explain this would be to find two charts and show how one eclipse affected them both. This story, however, not only affected the people concerned—it shocked the world.

On 13 December 1936, there was a solar eclipse at 22 degrees Sagittarius. This, of course, is related to the abdication of Edward VIII. The meaning of this eclipse is:

'**Suddenly deciding to make greater commitments in a relationship. This eclipse was gentle, and trust the situation that arises and allow themselves to be led by their momentum.**' (Bernadette Brady, *Predictive Astrology,* p. 323)

This eclipse fell in the 11th house of Edward VIII's natal chart—the house of hopes and wishes (Fig 2). So how did this eclipse affect his younger brother, George VI (Fig 3)? The Sun (☉) in his natal chart (the ruler of the Monarch) took a direct hit from this eclipse, as it fell close to his birthday, so his solar return picked up the eclipse as well. (A solar return is when the Sun returns to its birth position and sets up a new horoscope for one year.) To find out how this eclipse was going to affect him, you have to find the house that the Sun rules in the natal chart.

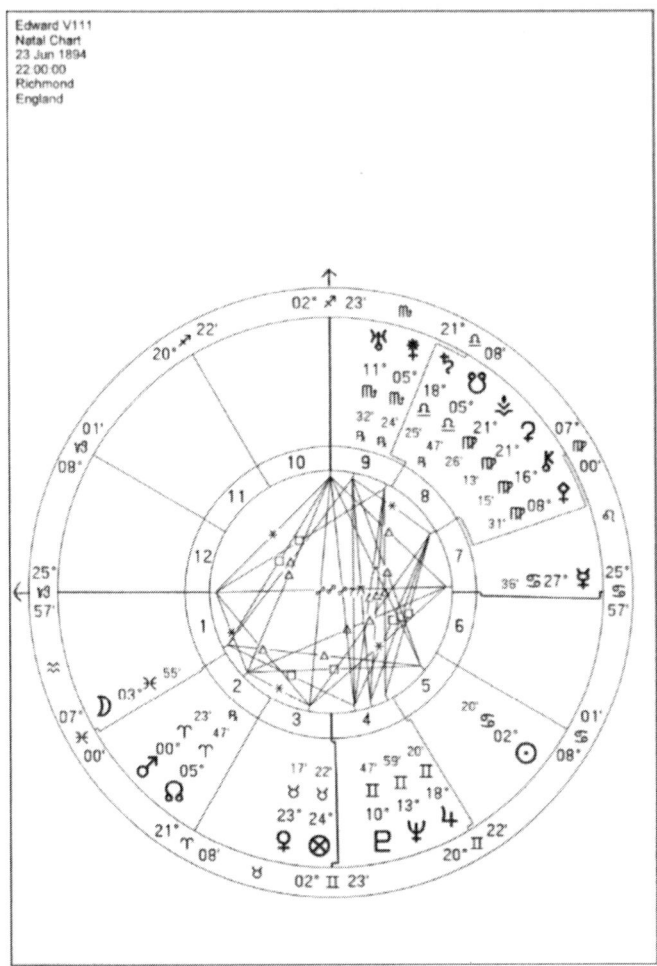

Fig 2

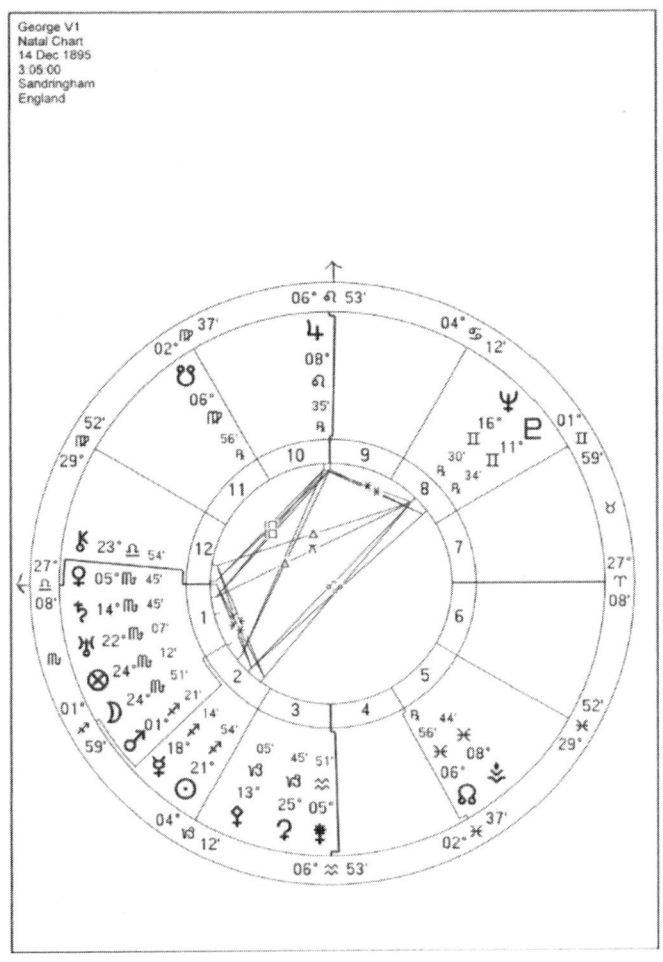

Fig 3

In the chart of George VI, it rules the 10th house of career and how the outside world sees you. Placed in the 10th house is the planet Jupiter (♃), the greater benefic, in the sign of Leo—the lion, the king. Even though George VI was the younger of the two brothers, it was his chart that was leading him to the throne.

The chart of Edward VIII has a debilitated Jupiter, so it would find it hard to achieve what it wanted. Jupiter (♃) rules his 10th and 11th houses, and this relates to him having to make a choice between becoming king and marrying Wallis Simpson. Although there was a great deal of upset in the Royal Family over this matter—not to mention among the palace staff and the rest of the country—astrology can have its way. But in this case, what was needed was a change to the system. This was to follow years later. This pill may have been easier to swallow if the Royal Household had known what was really going on behind the scenes.

'And the Moon into blood.'

When a lunar eclipse or full moon takes place, the Sun is opposite the Moon (Fig 4). The Moon's light is fully exposed, and it is at this time that things get exposed. Any secrets or information you wanted kept to yourself may well find themselves open to the public. Things come to an end—and in my case, this was certainly true.

On the 18/10/2013, a lunar eclipse occurred just before midnight. The Moon was in the 6th house of daily routine—this was about to change. The rule is: the house where you find the Moon will deliver an event—and it did. My marriage was over.

The house where you find the Sun is where the action is. The Sun was in the 12th house of hidden matters and secrets. The one important thing: the Sun (outside chart) was next to Neptune (Ψ) in the inside chart. Neptune rules my 5th house, which deals with love affairs but also estate agents.

That day, I quietly went to view a house. The eclipse took place that night. The next day I went back for a second viewing, unaware that an eclipse had taken place. I put in an offer, which was accepted. The lunar eclipse had done its job. It was over, and I was on my way to a new life.

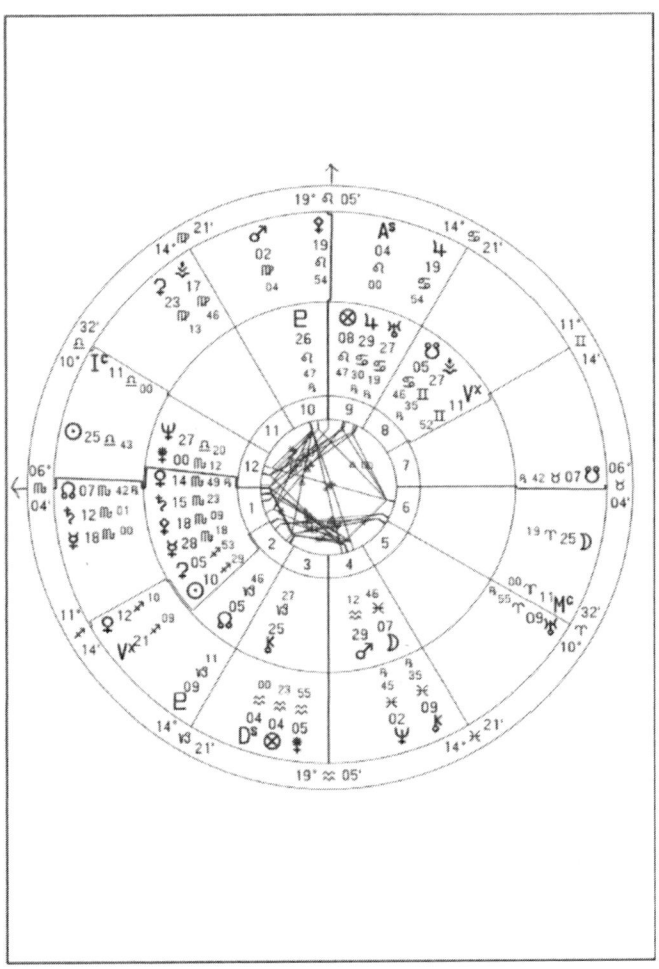

Fig 4

St Luke's Gospel, Chapter 21, Verses 7 & 25

Verse 7: And they asked him, saying, '**Master, when will these things be? And what sign will there be when these things come to pass?**'

Verse 25: Jesus replies, '**And there shall be signs in the Sun, and in the Moon, and in the Stars; and upon the earth distress of nations, with perplexity; the sea and the waters roaring.**'

As you can see, Jesus is asked a question, and in verse 25, He gives His reply.

There is another form of astrology known as *Horary Astrology*. This is used in the absence of a birth chart. During the reign of Charles II, there was an astrologer called William Lilly, who specialised in this field. He wrote a book called *Christian Astrology,* which is still in use today. It has never been translated into modern English for fear of losing its original meaning, so students have to get used to reading Old English, as I did.

Horary astrology is very useful. Questions can be asked on almost anything: relationships, buying or selling property, career—and the one I make the most use of—finding lost property. So I have included a chart showing how I found a lost crystal.

Before I start the judgement of this chart (Fig 5), two things need to be explained:

1. The signs of the zodiac are linked to compass directions.
2. When looking at a chart, you would expect to find NORTH at the top, but in fact, it is at the bottom. The compass points are as such:

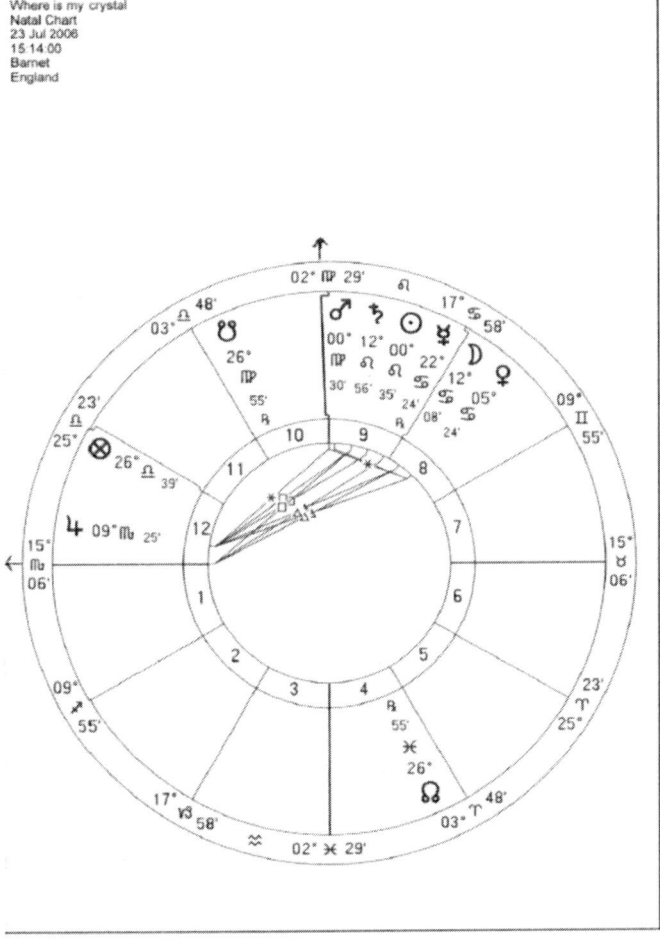

Fig 5

I have a small collection of crystals on display on the window ledge. Owing to the hot weather, the window was open, and two days before the chart was cast, I noticed one was missing. My greatest fear was it had fallen out of the window, causing considerable damage to my car parked outside.

After checking the drive, I came to the conclusion that the crystal was still in the house.

The Ascendant (1st house) is on the East side of the chart. Moving anti-clockwise, the 2nd house of movable possessions is ruled by Jupiter (♃), which is in the 12th house close to the Ascendant.

Mars (♂), my ruler, is at the top of the chart, close to the cusp of the 10th house, highlighting it. Mars is important in this chart, as it also rules the 6th house of routine, service, and small animals. Mars is making an aspect to Jupiter, which means I had to look harder. Mars is also next to the fixed star *Regulus*.

The Moon is within one degree of making an aspect to Mercury (☿), ruler of the 10th house, where Mars is located. The Moon is separating from Jupiter, which meant that at one point I had been very close to it—which I had.

Jupiter is in Scorpio, a water sign, which meant it was somewhere near a source of water. Mars is in Virgo, an earth sign. The radiator is under the window on the East side of the house. The 12th house is in the eastern quarter of heaven, so the crystal was near the window.

Later that night, I found it. The fact that Mars was angular provided the answer. The Ascendant and the 6th house are relevant in this case. Its position in Virgo (an earth sign) meant I had to look nearer the floor. It had fallen off the window ledge and landed in the cat's bed (Mars, the ruler of small animals), which is kept by the radiator under the window on the east wall.

Mars close to Regulus meant I would be successful. The Part of Fortune (⊗) is close to the fixed star *Spica* (which is helpful to the situation) and Mercury, the 10th house ruler. It is also in contact with the Sun.

'And there shall be signs in the Sun, and the Moon, and the Stars.'

Now that I have shown that the practice of astrology is nothing to be frightened of, why has the Church, since its beginning, tried—and succeeded—to keep this from the general public?

We are encouraged to read the Bible, yet the very book they try so hard to get us to read contains the astrology they don't want us to get involved with.

Astrology has also inspired musicians: Gustav Holst (an astrologer in his own right) with *The Planets* suite, and Joseph Haydn with the chorus from *The Creation*: 'The heavens are telling the glory of God.'

My feeling is that the world needs to wake up and embrace this subject. I am not suggesting for one moment that everyone needs to take up the study of astrology. But what I am suggesting is that everyone needs to be aware it is there. And in times of trouble or upheaval, you know where to go for answers.

After all, your birth chart was the first birthday present you were given. Don't discard it. I am sure if you gave a birthday present to someone you loved, and they gave it back to you saying they didn't want it—how would that make you feel?

Yet that's exactly what we have been made to do.

The rest I will leave for your own thoughts.

How to Set the Date for Easter

This may feel like a strange thing to include in an astrology book. I will give you three guesses where its origins lie. Firstly, we have to wait for the Spring Equinox, which falls around the 21st March, when the Sun moves into the sign of Aries and so begins the astrological year. Outside, the Earth is warming up, the flowers are blooming, and birds are busy building nests.

After this has taken place, the next thing is to wait for the following full moon, and the Sunday after that full moon will be Easter Sunday.

That's how you find it. But why?

The First Council of Nicaea in 325 AD laid down the rules for setting the date. They laid down only two: independence from the Jewish calendar and worldwide uniformity. This festival is based on a lunar cycle. My question here is: did they simply set this system up, or did they know there was a connection between a full moon and St John's Gospel?

This is only symbolic, but it does have great significance when it comes to the timing of the festival.

The chart I have included is a secondary progressed chart (Fig 6), with the outer ring showing the progressed positons and inner ring showing the natal chart. If you look at the outer ring, you will see the Sun (☉) and Moon (☽) are exactly opposite each other. In a secondary progressed chart, these moon phases occur once every 30 years. This is personal to the chart holder, and it will be felt.

A full moon signifies the culmination of something. Whatever it is won't grow anymore. And in this case, that's exactly what happened.

This chart belongs to me, and this full moon brought an end to my career and the beginning of another—none of which I expected or really wanted. But that's astrology for you. At this point, I hadn't even considered studying astrology. That was to follow eight years later.

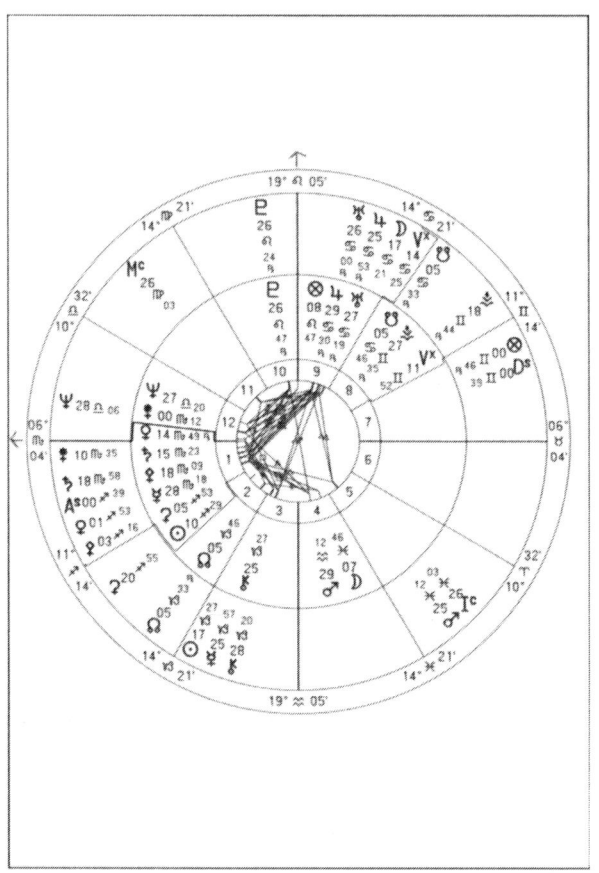

Fig 6

This was a hard pill to swallow. If I had been aware of what was going on in the background, it would have been easier when seeing events unfold on a piece of paper.

Having explained the meaning of the full moon, why is it linked to a religious festival? If you read the Easter story in all four Gospels, you will find that St John's Gospel (Chapter 10, Verse 30) is worded differently. In this account, Jesus says, **'It is finished.'** Did the Council of Nicaea select a full moon for the timing of Easter for this reason? Any moon phase could have been chosen, but a full moon is significant. If they did, then again, astrology has found a way into religion. There is also a connection to the Jewish festival of Passover.

Part 2

Chapter 3
The Ages

All planets have a fixed time when they return to the place where they were at the time of your birth. This is known as a *return*. People are often unaware of this, but in the case of the Sun, everyone knows—it's your birthday. When the Sun returns to its birth position, it sets up a chart known as a *Solar Return*, which forecasts the next twelve months. This return occurs the day before, on, or the day after your birthday, hence the saying, 'Many happy returns'. So many people say this, but I wonder how many know its origins.

The Moon
The Moon takes twenty-eight days to return to its birth position and sets up a *Lunar Return*. This return shows how you are going to function on an emotional level, and the house the Moon is placed in is where your feelings will be strongest.

Mercury
Mercury takes approximately one year to make its return. A new chart can be cast to see how your thoughts, communications and creative skills will be used over the next

twelve months. The house placement will again highlight the area of life where these skills will be applied. Some examples:

- *Seventh house:* communication skill through relationships.
- Fifth house: creativity—perhaps writing a book.

Venus

Venus is a social planet; it also deals with beauty. If you find Venus in the fourth house of a return chart, you may decide to redecorate your home. In the eleventh, you could be in for a fun time with friends or group activities.

Age 2

Mars has a two-year orbit. This is where the saying *the terrible twos* comes from. When a child reaches the age of two, Mars returns to its birth position. This transit sets off a change in children, much to their parents' frustration. To understand this, you need to know what Mars symbolises: energy, aggression, war, independence, sport, and assertiveness.

Something is happening here under the surface. When a child reaches the age of two, they have already started to make some sense of the world around them, and they begin to put up a barrier between themselves and their parents. This is all about achieving some form of independence, and this is when the tantrums start. This, of course, can be a dangerous time, as they may get into all sorts of scrapes. It is a natural part of growing up. Some children find it hard to handle the energy. The best way of coping is to find out if there is a leaning towards any sporting activity that can provide a safe outlet for any excess energy.

Age 7

At the age of seven, Saturn will have moved thirty degrees from its birth position, forming an aspect known as a *square*. This can be a bit challenging. The Saturn square is associated with physical changes: children lose their milk teeth and grow adult teeth. Psychologically, another barrier is coming down.

Saturn is known as the *schoolteacher of the zodiac*. Its life lessons can sometimes be difficult. It also enforces discipline and responsibility but can also bring obstruction and delays. It grounds us and establishes boundaries. All of this shapes our personality and the way we take responsibility in our adult lives.

Age 15

Saturn hasn't finished yet. At the age of fifteen, Saturn reaches its *opposition point*. This, of course, coincides with adolescence, school exams and a planet enforcing more responsibility and discipline. No wonder teenagers have trouble.

Again, there is a break for more independence—wanting to be with friends on a shopping trip rather than with their parents. We are at the point where Saturn makes us grow up. It can shake us out of our comfort zone and makes us tackle issues we would rather leave to someone else or forget about. For a fifteen-year-old, the schoolteacher of the zodiac is cracking the whip: 'You need to start revising if you want to pass your exams.' We have all been there!

Age 30

At the age of thirty, Saturn makes its first return to its natal position. Many people feel they are getting old, as they have said goodbye to their twenties. This first return can bring with it responsibility of a different kind. This may come in the form of marriage and settling down, or, for those already settled, the arrival of their first baby. A different approach to work may be needed. Some find themselves promoted to a managerial position.

To find out where responsibility lies, locate the house where Saturn falls in the natal chart. Whichever house Saturn falls in, there seems to lurk a degree of fear. Some examples:

In the 7th house, relationships could be a problem.

In the 5th, creativity could take on a serious approach, and the fun may be taken out of the scenario.

Someone with Saturn in the 10th will go all out to enhance their career once they have overcome any fear of not being able to do so.

This will, of course, depend on how Saturn is aspected by the rest of the chart.

Age 40–42

Somewhere between forty and forty-two, Uranus reaches the halfway point around the chart. It has an eighty-four-year orbit, so by the early forties, it is opposite its natal position. This is known as the *midlife crisis*. It is at this point that major changes can take place, whether they are wanted or not.

Some see this transit as a crisis in their lives, and if they are unable to cope with the situation, seeking outside help usually follows. This can come in the form of counselling, consulting a psychologist, or speaking with a doctor.

What they don't know is that their chart is telling them something. The problem is, all these agencies don't know the source of the problem. The big planets don't make changes for fun; this is all about development and following a path. And if any planet will push you into accepting change, Uranus will. It doesn't do it quietly; there is always an upheaval.

What you will experience will depend on where your natal Uranus is placed. The transiting Uranus will be in the house opposite, setting off a reaction across the axis. So if natal Uranus is in the 9th house (faith, philosophy, higher education or travel), the transiting Uranus will activate that position when it reaches the 3rd house. This may not be so dramatic. There may be a sudden desire to take up some form of study. In my case, it was the study of astrology, and I bought my first computer. Uranus deals with technology. The 2nd and 8th houses may bring on financial issues. The 4th and 10th, home and career. The 5th and 11th, creativity, hobbies, friends and groups.

Always remember: when something happens that you don't like or that upsets the balance of your life, there is always a reason for it. It may not be apparent at the time, but one day you will look back and say, 'So that is why that happened'. And the answer will always be found in your chart. The problem is, people don't know where to look for the answer.

There will be more on the behaviour of Uranus in the next chapter.

Age 58–60: Second Saturn Return

Between the ages of 58 and 60, Saturn will return to its natal position for the second time. It is at this point in our lives that we start to think of retirement and how we want to spend the rest of our lives.

At the first Saturn return, thirty years earlier, we learnt how to take on responsibility for home and work. We had to put down boundaries and create a structure that enabled us to function both at home and at work.

At the second return, things are about to change. For those who are able to retire and whose children may have left home, a great deal of this structure is gone. Some experience the 'empty nest' syndrome, as their daily routine has disappears overnight. It is at this point that we have to lay a new form of routine and structure for ourselves. We now have the time to revisit those hobbies and interests we once had, but had to shelve because of other commitments. This will now enable us to plan for the future.

Chapter 4
What Makes You Think We Can Tell You

It's an understood fact that when clients consult an astrologer, the main purpose of their visit is to find out what the future holds. Many think that an astrologer can predict the future, and to a certain degree, they can see what events are being presented. These events are being produced by the houses in a chart being activated. Planets in a house receiving transits, eclipses and moon phases will be affected. The ancient astrologers used a method of chart turning. This added numerous events to each house, to the point where a chart could have in region of 144 different connotations. So, with this scenario, it would be impossible to pinpoint a specific event. The astrologer can certainly say that this house is being activated and that you can expect action in this area of life. The other issue for the astrologer to deal with is that many people think once a chart has been activated, whatever follows has to be, and many have said that their freedom of choice has been taken away. Once a chart starts to produce an event, the client is left with a choice of whether they do or whether they don't.

Change

Some events in our lives will occur outside our control. On many occasions, they can bring about major changes, and usually, it's change we could do well without. Some of these changes can be devastating, but it's how we deal with the situation before us that matters. These changes are for the development of the soul, so we can grow spiritually and move forward.

These changes usually come under the influence of the slower planets. Once they start activating the natal chart, you can be sure that, once they have passed, things won't be the same as before. All the chart holder can do is go with the flow and be guided to a new course of action. There is no point in trying to fight it and force a situation to return to what it was. What was has passed; it now needs to be let go of, in order to allow what is waiting to materialise.

We will have a look at the outer planets and see how this happens.

Uranus

The planet Uranus was discovered in 1781 by William Herschel. It is erratic in its behaviour, as it is in its orbit. It takes 84 years to orbit the Sun just once. It delivers its message of change through sudden events, shock and surprises, causing chaos and disruption. It rules the sign of Aquarius, along with its traditional ruler, Saturn.

So, let's have a look at what can happen when Uranus arrives at the 10th house cusp, which rules your career (Fig 7). The natal placement is in the 4th house.

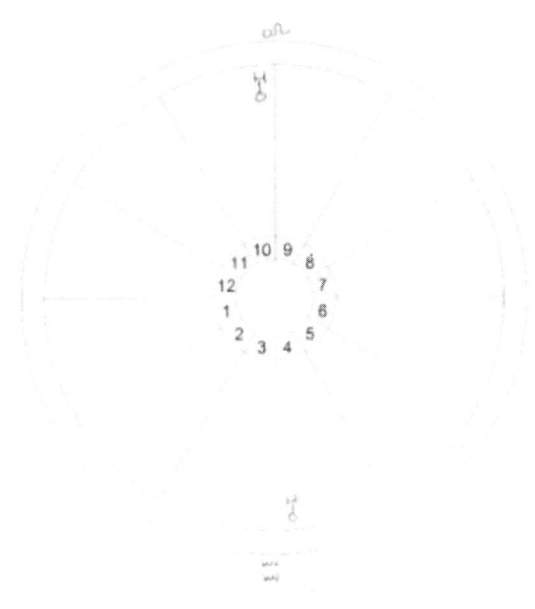

Fig 7

This could bring major changes to your career as you know it.

1. Your boss could announce redundancies, and the impact will be felt at home, as Aquarius rules the house of home in this chart.

Looking a little deeper into this situation, something is occurring outside your control—but is it as bad as it seems? After the initial shock of what has happened, people often find themselves looking at retraining for a different career or setting up their own business.

Retraining for a new career can unlock hidden talents that may not have been realised. Starting your own business in an area different from what you have been doing before will have the same effect, but with the added responsibility of being the boss and in control of all aspects, including the finances. Saturn, the traditional ruler of Aquarius, will have an influence in this.

So, without the initial shock of losing your job in the first place, none of this would have happened. This is how change works: you first have to let go before something new arrives. Without the letting go, we carry on with the same routine and get stuck in a rut.

Neptune

Neptune works very differently. Its quiet approach will gradually break down a structure through erosion. You may feel you are losing your grip on a situation in certain areas of life. Your boundaries are being broken down, and while this process is taking place, you could come into contact with new situations you never thought possible. So, let's place a transiting Neptune passing through your 5th house (Fig 8). The 5th house deals with your creativity, hobbies, love affairs, and children, if applicable. One or more of these areas could be subject to change.

Let's take your creativity and hobbies. You may find that an instrument you have always wanted to play slowly starts to manifest. Neptune deals with music. You start finding the time to learn and practice, and what first started as a daunting process loses its grip on difficulty, and the music starts to flow from within you. On some occasions, your music may change, and you can take on another instrument and expand your repertoire. This could also be a time when writing can flow. Ideas may be numerous, and plays, books, and music can be easier to produce. For the time while Neptune is passing through, the boundaries that held you back are slowly disintegrating.

The same can be said for any house Neptune enters. Your 10th house can see a gradual dissatisfaction with your career. You slowly start to see that changes are needed, and this could be the time for a complete change. Or, if you are approaching retirement, this might not be as daunting as you once thought. We lose our grip on what we once thought important, allowing something new to materialise.

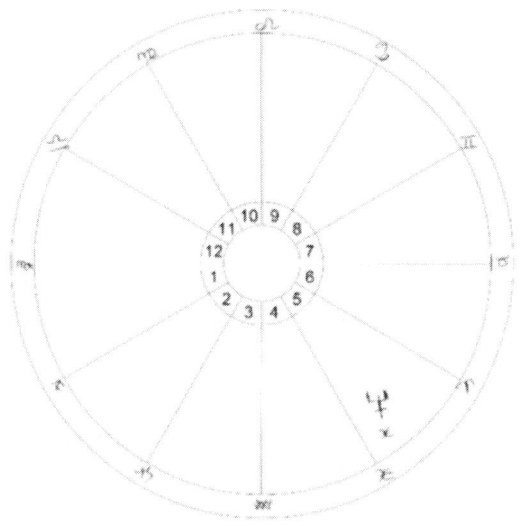

Fig 8

Pluto

We have now arrived at the last of the slow planets in our solar system. Having said that, in 2006 Pluto lost its status as a planet and became a dwarf planet. Regardless of what the astronomers think, to give or remove status has little or no impact on the potency of Pluto.

When Pluto starts to make an application to your Sun, or any of the angular houses, it won't go unnoticed. Pluto's job is to cleanse, clear and expose what is hidden before change can take place. Its movement is very slow, so change can take years to complete. Something will have to go before this can happen.

Pluto's method of change is different from that of Uranus and Neptune. It's like a volcano that starts to rumble and gradually intensifies until there is an eruption. The events can come from the outside, of which you have no control, or an internal dissatisfaction until finally you can take no more.

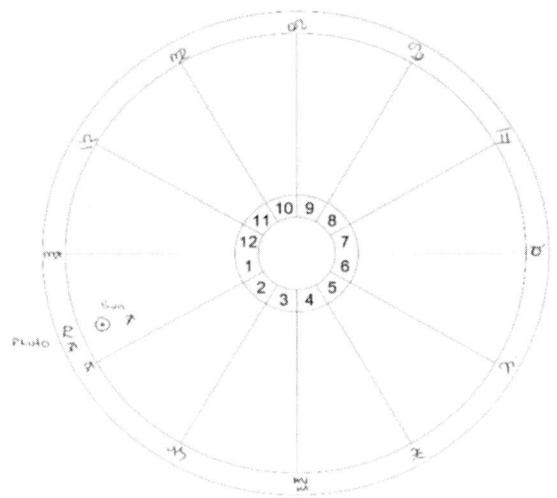

Fig 9

The house that Pluto is moving through is the area of life that is affected. If Pluto crosses the Sun in your chart, it's you who will eventually change, although it can take many years for this to happen. Any other planet that Pluto comes into contact with from anywhere in the chart will be affected and modify the meaning of this change. It can bring others into your story.

This is how a Pluto transit affected me. My Sun is in Sagittarius. Pluto started to make its approach in 1997 (Fig 9). At the end of February that year, I lost a close friend of mine. This was sudden and totally unexpected, but this sowed the seeds of a major change in me and set on the road to becoming an astrologer.

The asteroid Chiron is the wounded healer; its symbol is a key. Taking both our charts, my Chiron is on her Ascendant; it's as though she is holding the key to my future. While Pluto moved back and forth over my Sun, I started studying astrology, and in 2002 passed the first set of exams. In 2009, I completed a Diploma in Traditional Astrology.

I started working with clients, attending mind, body and soul events, taking workshops, and giving talks at astrology groups, as well as doing client work—but Pluto still hadn't finished with me.

The conclusion to this story is in the chapter headed *The Nodes of the Moon*.

Chapter 5
The Planets

It is not my intention to produce a cookbook of planets, signs and houses as there are numerous books to choose from, but I will give a short explanation of what they represent. I have already spoken about the outer planets—Uranus, Neptune and Pluto—so I will concentrate on the remaining seven: Sun, Moon, Mercury, Venus, Mars, Jupiter and Saturn.

The Sun (☉)

The Sun sign you have is the journey for this lifetime. You are here to learn about the characteristics of your Sun sign and to achieve its meaning. This can take a lifetime. You are only one twelfth of a whole. This is your piece of divine fire—your ego. So now I will take you through the signs and explain what you need to achieve. The Sun's metal is gold; its gender is male, and it is hot and dry.

Sun in Aries

Here you are to learn about creative energy and enthusiasm. This sign is about getting projects started. Fast-acting and energetic, Aries doesn't hang around. Its one problem is that it may not stay around long enough to see things finished—it wants to move on to the next adventure.

Sun in Taurus

Here you are required to become efficient in practical matters. Taurus asks that you develop a love for the Earth you live on. Gardening is one activity that this sign leans towards.

Sun in Gemini

Communication is the lesson here. Acquisition of knowledge is another requirement. Gemini is a busy sign—multitasking seems to be a talent. People with this sign get bored easily, so mental stimulation is a must.

Sun in Cancer

This sign is to do with nurturing, care for others and home. Emotional security is very important. People with this sign need a secure home life and will strive to make it so.

Sun in Leo

This sign teaches how to be generous of heart and develop a sense of integrity. This kingly sign will develop a sense of pride in what we do.

Sun in Virgo

This sign is about developing efficiency. Work needs to be carried out carefully, paying attention to detail. However, there can also be a tendency to be too picky, which can lead to a lack of spontaneity.

Sun in Libra

The sign of the scales—which need to be balanced. People born under this sign need to maintain the status quo and care for themselves as well as others. This can be difficult, as they tend to give to others and ignore their own needs.

Sun in Scorpio

This sign is about transformation. Here, the chart holder is to learn how to dig into the unknown. Some areas of work involve research, detection or occult investigations.

Sun in Sagittarius

This sign requires you to develop skills of honesty, straightforwardness and forward thinking—represented by the arrow flying swiftly to its goal.

Sun in Capricorn

Here you are required to develop skills of organisation. Ambition is also a trait of this sign. However, for some, this may not come easily, as they may feel they are not good enough and can lack self-confidence.

Sun in Aquarius

This time around, you will be seeking freedom—not wanting to be tied down. You will also, on some level, develop humanitarian skills along with a need for friends.

Sun in Pisces

This is the last of the signs. A Sun in Pisces is here to learn about empathy and sympathy for the feelings of others.

The Moon (☽)

The Moon in your chart shows how you respond to the outside world on an emotional level. The house where you find it is the area of life that means a lot to you and where you satisfy your needs. The Moon rules the sign of Cancer, and its metal is silver. It is cold and moist, and its gender is female.

Moon in Aries

This placement can make you emotionally volatile and impulsive. It doesn't take much to make you angry, but once you have made your feelings known, it soon blows over and is forgotten.

Moon in Taurus

There is a need to be emotionally, financially and materially secure. Food is of great importance here, too.

Moon in Gemini

Emotional security is brought on by the need to communicate with others. People with this placement may take up teaching or some form of public work where they can speak for others.

Moon in Cancer

Here, in its own sign, there is a strong emotional personality. Home and family are important. When hurt or upset, these individuals will retreat into their shell.

Moon in Leo

This is someone who is a proud person—this pride will satisfy their emotional needs. They love being in the spotlight, which can lead them into a public career. Many actors have this placement.

Moon in Virgo

Emotional satisfaction is brought about through hard work, neatness, cleanliness and good housekeeping. They are also concerned with health. There can be a tendency to overanalyse their feelings, which can lead to a loss of spontaneity.

Moon in Libra

Emotionally, they need to maintain a balance in relationships. Their emotional well-being depends on the approval of others, and they can neglect their own needs to maintain harmony.

Moon in Scorpio

Very strong emotions are present here. They take their personal affairs very seriously, but the downside can lead to jealousy and possessiveness.

Moon in Sagittarius

Light-hearted with a good sense of humour, but they may lack a realistic view of life due to setting their goals too high.

Moon in Capricorn

This can give the appearance of being cold and austere. Their emotional nature is reserved and cautious. Everything is taken seriously; they identify with the material and may let go of spiritual values.

Moon in Aquarius

The song 'Born Free' comes to mind here. There is no point trying to pin someone down with this placement—if you try, they will just take off. However, they can gain a great deal of emotional satisfaction by working for a humanitarian cause.

Moon in Pisces

Like the Sun in Pisces, here we have a very sensitive emotional nature. These individuals can walk into a room and immediately pick up on the atmosphere. This can lead to strong psychic abilities.

Mercury (☿)

Mercury, otherwise known as Hermes, is the planet of communication. This is the winged messenger—with wings on his helmet and feet. With this planet, there is a need to satisfy and forge links between others. The personality is fun-loving, quick-thinking and inventive.

Mercury has rulership over communication, travel, modes of transport, the traditional ruler of computers, internet, phones, e-mails and post. Mercury indicates how you think and communicate, and this is reflected through the astrological sign in which it is situated. This reveals your ability to make decisions and deductions. The house position shows the area of life that is most influenced by the information you gather.

Mercury is cold and dry, and it is considered hermaphroditic. It takes on the nature of any planet it is close to. Its metal is quicksilver—cold and dry but convertible.

Mercury is the first planet to enter what is known as a retrograde phase. This occurs three times a year, each lasting about three weeks. This phase is when the planet appears to be moving backwards in space. It's not—but the Earth is pulling away from it, giving that impression. This phase doesn't go unnoticed by astrologers. It has the ability to cause a great deal of disruption to daily life.

Taking into account what Mercury rules, it's obvious where the chaos will ensue. So let's go back to December 2016. Mercury went retrograde on the 19th of December. Southern Railways were on strike, there were problems at the airports, and staff were planning action on Christmas and Boxing Day. Just to add to the mix, the postal service joined in, stating there could be delays with the post.

These are the sorts of antics that go on at this time. It is also likely that there could be computer problems. However, there are some good points to this phase—it's very useful for exam revision. It gives you time to think or re-think any ideas you have.

I can remember, as an astrology student, our exams had been set during a Mercury retrograde phase. We all thought our tutors had lost the plot—but we were wrong. It certainly helped with the concentration. And yes, I passed.

So, let's have a look at Mercury through the signs.

Mercury in Aries

Quick thinking, and may wish to charge headlong into activities without much thought at all.

Mercury in Taurus

This is someone who will take time to make up their mind on anything, and once this is done, they won't change their mind easily.

Mercury in Gemini

This is one of the signs Mercury rules. Again, this will be someone who is quick-thinking, needing a variety of activities on the go at the same time. The mind needs to be kept active, as boredom sets in easily. This is a versatile placement—more concerned about facts than the attitudes of others. Able to communicate easily in speech and writing.

Mercury in Cancer

The mind works here on a deep-seated emotional patterns. Home and family can be the main focus of their thoughts. In business, they may lean towards working in real estate or consumer products.

Mercury in Leo

Someone with a strong mind and fixed purpose. There is mental self-confidence here, and this makes for a positive attitude when tackling and solving problems—but they are prone to miss out on the details. Areas of special interest are the theatre, an ability in teaching and mental development of children.

Mercury in Virgo

This is the other sign that Mercury rules, but Mercury placed here is very different from Mercury in Gemini. There is an analytical approach to most tasks. Minute precision and accuracy are the order of the day—through this can appear to be trivial to others. They need orderly surroundings and efficient ways of working. Scientific work and research come to mind.

Mercury in Libra

This placement requires a mind that is concerned with relationships. There is a strong curiosity about the behaviour patterns of others. To put this into practice, they lean towards psychology, astrology, public relations, sociology and law. Good communication and happiness in relationships are important. There is a strong sense of harmony and justice. On the downside, they find it difficult to make up their own mind—swinging from one side of the scale to the other.

Mercury in Scorpio

Here lies a deep, probing mind. This placement is good for investigating. They need to get to the root of the matter before applying any form of solution. They can be blunt or even sharp with their language. They are either outspoken or keep silent. This placement makes good detectives and researchers.

Mercury in Sagittarius

Mercury in this sign gives concern for social thought—an interest in education, religion and philosophy. Law and travel may also be important. Anyone with Mercury here can very blunt, they will tell it how it is. There is a need for mental freedom. They always think ahead—usually with a good sense of humour.

Mercury in Capricorn

Mercury gives an organised mind. Their thoughts can be ambitious, practical and shrewd. They take one step at a time, and their reasoning process is thorough. They can develop mathematical ability owing to discipline and patience. Many executives have this placement, as they have good managerial ability.

Mercury in Aquarius

Free-thinking and open to new ideas. The truth always comes first with this position. They don't have much time for the traditional ways of doing things—out with the old and in with the new. In relationships, they don't worry too much about what is expected of them. They will follow their own thought patterns, not caring what others think.

Mercury in Pisces

This placement gives a vivid imagination. They can be highly intuitive and telepathic. They pick up on the thoughts and moods of others. Arriving at conclusions through logical reasoning is not their style—they rely more on intuitive perception. They can be sympathetic, as they can imagine what it's like to be in someone else's shoes. They are open to daydreaming and woolgathering, and making up their mind can be a challenge, owing to the symbol of Pisces: two fish swimming in opposite directions.

Venus (♀)

Venus deals with love, art, beauty and the principles of relationships. This planet is closest in size to Earth. It is a very inhospitable planet—it has boiling hot clouds of sulphuric acid—and the connection with love is how much pain can be endured because of it.

The sign you find Venus in shows how someone expresses their emotions. Venus is connected to the arts, music and beauty. An example: Venus found in the fourth house of home and roots will express itself as someone who wants a beautiful home.

Its nature is cold and moist, its metal is copper and its gender is female.

Venus is Aries

Someone who comes across forcefully in their expression. Can be competitive and aggressive when seeking the affections of others, and can be impulsive, requiring a great deal of attention.

Venus in Taurus

This is the first sign that Venus rules. Here, Venus gives long-lasting affections. Beauty is also important. As Taurus is an earth sign, this placement produces good gardeners, beautifying the earth. As Venus deals with music, when placed in Taurus, it tends to give rich, melodious voices.

Venus in Gemini

This brings a love of travelling and artistic expression. Jokes can be a source of fun, especially if there is a play on words. They like variety in their romantic lives. There is a curiosity about people, which can cause a difficulty in settling down.

Venus in Cancer

These people are deeply sensitive in their romantic lives. They can be easily hurt but hide this vulnerability. They seek a stable domestic life—marriage is important—as is the wish to create a safe and beautiful home. If the planet is not well-aspected, there is a tendency to sulk.

Venus in Leo

Their behaviour can be quite theatrical, especially in areas of love. They make good actors. They have a warm-hearted and sunny personality. They like to show off their partner but can be possessive or jealous if not paid the proper attention.

Venus in Virgo

This is a difficult placement for Venus. There is a tendency to over-analyse feelings and be very critical of those they love. Always looking for the perfect partner, they can scupper their own happiness by not accepting people for who they are—flaws and all. They may also block the spontaneous flow of affection. Their work can often be in artistic fields or beauty parlours of some description.

Venus in Libra

This is the other sign that Venus rules, but it acts differently from its rulership of Taurus. Venus in Libra wants harmony in all relationships. They have the ability to understand the feelings of others and a strong desire to please. Unlike Venus in Taurus, which seeks status through money and possessions, Venus in Libra seeks status through relationships, often making money through their pleasing manner when dealing with the public.

Venus in Scorpio

Venus in Scorpio produces a strong, passionate person, prone to jealousy and secrecy. Their emotions are very intense and sometimes prevent the acceptance of other people's point of view. They can sacrifice everything for love if they feel their significant other is worth it.

Venus in Sagittarius

There is an idealistic and spiritual response with this placement—a welcome light relief from the sign that precedes it. They can be outspoken about their feelings and have traditional moral structures that make them feel secure. They are honest about their feelings. Artistically, they may display flamboyant use of colours. Outdoor activities can include sports, horse riding, camping and hiking. There can also be a love of religious music.

Venus in Capricorn

Here, Venus wishes to work for material status to achieve security. This may include rising to a position of authority in any chosen field. They are dignified and reserved in public, which can sometimes be mistaken for snobbishness. However, in private, they are capable of being very tender.

Venus in Aquarius

Aquarius gives rise to someone who wants to be friends with everyone but not necessarily settle down. Adhering to the standard rules laid down by society is not easy for them—they have their own interpretation of what is meaningful. They find crude behaviour unacceptable. Romantic relationships are often sudden and can end as quickly as they began. Intellectual stimulation is important—they can't survive boring relationships. They also need to socialise and have many friends. They may be interested in unusual forms of art.

Venus in Pisces

Venus functions very well in this sign. It brings the principle of love to its highest evolutionary development. People with this placement marry for love—other considerations have no place here. There is deep compassion and sympathy, verging on spirituality. A sense of eternal life flows through all things, uniting the soul with the universe. They understand the feelings of others and know what it is like to walk in someone else's shoes. They can draw on a higher dimension for artistic and musical outlets.

Mars (♂)

According to Gustave Holst, who wrote The Planets suite, Mars is the bringer of war—and aptly named. This planet is all about energy—your get-up-and-go. Its metal is iron, it's hot and dry, and its gender is male.

Mars in Aries

There is an uncontainable energy here, which must have a safe outlet if there is to be a peaceful existence. Otherwise, this can lead to aggression and violence. People can lack staying power—often at the forefront of initiation, but they lose interest and move on to other projects. This behaviour pattern follows through with most of the personal planets in Aries. Aries is the first sign that Mars rules.

Mars in Taurus

Mars in Taurus has a bit of difficulty maintaining speed of action, as it is placed in the opposite sign of Scorpio—the second sign Mars rules. Mars in Taurus is slowed down; this, however, can give great determination and perseverance once a course of action has been decided upon. As the sign of Taurus deals with beauty and craftsmanship, this placement can lead to the creation of work and precision in the use of tools. If gardening is the chosen outlet, a great deal of work can go into this.

Mars in Gemini

The sign of Gemini deals with our communication skills. Mars here can certainly liven up any debate, and anything that is intellectual can become a contest. There can be ingenuity and resourcefulness, but this can turn into a state of being argumentative and irritable. Occupations can lead to reporters, critics and journalists. There can be many changes of occupation, as Mars is restless in this sign.

Mars in Cancer

Mars does not function well in this sign. The element for Cancer is water, and it deals with emotions. This placement can be very emotional, which spills into anger if anything upsets the status quo. If the anger is supressed, psychological problems in later life may arise. An outlet for any pent-up problems is to put their energy into something creative—usually DIY around the home. There is also a need to own and run their own home. Women with this placement will fight to defend their families, but may in later life find it hard to let their children go, which can lead to jealousy.

Mars in Leo

This placement can produce someone who is self-confident. There is a stable side to the sign of Leo. Energy, willpower and creativity are highlighted here. Acting or leadership roles could manifest, as they have the ability to create self-confidence in others.

Mars in Virgo

Virgo is the sign that deals with health, so Mars placed here give skills in craftsmanship and precision. This placement can be found in the charts of surgeons, as Mars has a connection to knives. Action is planned very carefully and carried out systematically. They make strong perfectionists and on occasions, this gets in the way and nothing gets done at all. Their working environment needs to be well organised. There can be a nervous irritability here.

Mars in Libra

As the sign of Libra is about balance, there is a strong urge for action in a social context. Mars here is hampered by this position and will require approval and cooperation of others. Mars in Libra is not a bad position, as the sign of Libra is about balance and harmony—but Mars is one of aggressiveness and can be selfish, so in Libra, this behaviour is toned down. Their anger can spill out if they come across social injustice, even if they are not directly affected.

Mars in Scorpio

Scorpio is the second sign Mars rules. This is about powerful emotions and intensity. They can meet difficult situations with courage and resourcefulness. They find it hard to compromise and can be secretive about plans or actions.

Mars in Sagittarius

'Hellfire and damnation preacher' comes to mind here, especially if Mars is in contact with Mercury. Sagittarius, being the sign related to religion, attracts a great number with this placement will put their energy into the church. Sagittarius is also linked to outdoor pursuits, so activities such as sports or camping will be enjoyed. They can be very direct in their attitudes, but there is also a sense of fair play.

Mars in Capricorn

Mars functions very well here. There is a strong desire to be recognised for something. Energy is channelled into climbing the professional ladder. They organise themselves and anything they do to achieve their goals is carefully calculated. If they are keen on creating something, the building trade could be a possibility. They may not see themselves dancing to anyone else's tune, but are likely to end up being the one in charge.

Mars in Aquarius

As Mars is all about action, placed in Aquarius this can be brought about by unorthodox methods. There is a strong desire for freedom and independence. Good at organising and possessing a superior level of intelligence, add this all together and you have a person who needs to do things their own way. Their work can lead to engineering, electrical or mechanical placements. If they make good use of their energy, this can lead to humanitarian work through inventive and scientific achievements. Astrology can be an outlet they put their energy into.

Mars in Pisces

Self-confidence can be hampered in this sign. Mars is not an emotional planet, and placed in a water sign, there is a lack of energy. As Pisces deals with the unconscious, old resentments can be harboured. They need to learn not to brood over the past. For those with this position, they work best behind the scenes. If the horoscope supplies help from the Sun, Saturn, Uranus or Pluto, then this can help the Mars energy; otherwise, strength will be lacking.

Jupiter (♃)

The bringer of jollity, and the largest planet in our solar system. This is the planet of expansion—everything it does, it does in a big way. Should Jupiter be close to the Ascendant, it's our waistline that will expand. Its metal is tin; it is hot and moist, and its gender is male.

Jupiter in Aries

As this sign deals with leadership and action, Jupiter placed here adds the philosophical and spiritual dimensions to the sign—spiritual creativity. These people will exert positive action into spiritual, social and educational conditions. They have faith that they can contribute to a better way of life.

Jupiter in Taurus

Jupiter carries the spiritual way of life that will act differently through the signs. In Taurus, it's concerned with the best way to direct material resources and money. They are aware that these resources are loaned to us for the service of humanity. There is an ability here for business through patience and steadiness.

Jupiter in Gemini

There is a love of philosophy and study here. They wish to expand the mind through lines of communication, travel, social contact and study. Business can be connected with developing new ideas.

Jupiter in Cancer

From early childhood, generosity, kindness and religious and moral principles are installed via the home environment. Later, as they grow, these characteristics will be a part of their natural expression. Their homes can be used for religious or educational activities.

Jupiter in Leo

Leo is the sign of self-confidence and, with Jupiter placed here, this comes in abundance. This placement comes with honour, honesty and generosity. One of their concerns is the moral development of children. Their artistic interests could be in the entertainment industry. They make good teachers or spiritual counsellors.

Jupiter in Virgo

This position can pose difficulties. Virgo is the sign of precision and detail, while all Jupiter wants to do is to expand. This can result in overworking. If involved in a project, they must learn to delegate and enlist help from others or scale down their endeavours.

Jupiter in Libra
There is a strong need for justice here, along with moral principles in marriage, partnership and relationships. Any such union will be based on spiritual values, along with cooperation on a social scale. People with this placement can be efficient fundraisers for churches or charities.

Jupiter in Scorpio
As Jupiter is connected to philosophy and religion, placed in the sign of Scorpio, interests can move into the area of the mystical. Life after death and telepathic communication are usual—this is prominent if Jupiter makes contact with Uranus, Neptune or Pluto. They can be uncompromising about their religious beliefs, conduct and principles, and they can make some bitter enemies.

Jupiter in Sagittarius
Now in one of the signs it rules, there can be an outgoing personality with a love of philosophy, religion, education and travel. They have a far-sighted outlook on life, owing to the arrow indicated in the glyph for Sagittarius. They can see the big picture, which leads to a prophetic insight into the future.

Jupiter in Capricorn
Jupiter is about ethics. In Capricorn, and well–aspected, there can be great integrity when dealing in business matters and the responsibilities of high office. In the world of politics, they have traditional values and moral conduct. Jupiter is not

well-situated in this sign—its natural behaviour is to expand, but conditions here are limited. However, they can lean towards being prudent, cautious and of good, sound judgement.

Jupiter in Aquarius

Because of the freedom issues related to Aquarius, Jupiter placed here has no ties to religious, racial or class distinctions. Instead, they require social and moral values that are impartial in every respect and will need to share this with others. They can tolerate and understand that not all can live the same lifestyle or have the same set of values. They relate to the freedoms of the individual, both spiritually and evolutionarily.

Jupiter in Pisces

This is the second sign that Jupiter rules traditionally (before Neptune was discovered), but Jupiter still has rulership here. With Jupiter in this sign, there is emotional depth, with understanding and compassion. They have concerns for those less fortunate than themselves, working for charities or hospitals. There is a degree of mysticism here, and religious convictions can be emotional. There can be a psychic ability, especially if Jupiter aspects Uranus, Neptune or Pluto.

Saturn (♄)

Old Father Time, Saturn is the last planet that can be seen with the naked eye. Before the invention of the telescope, astronomers thought that Saturn was the last planet in our solar system. In astrology, Saturn usually gets bad press. It's known as the schoolteacher of the zodiac, and some of its lessons are hard, depressing and restrictive. But for all that, if we didn't have Saturn in our lives, there would be no structure, nothing to stop us from going too far, and no form of self-discipline. It takes approximately 30 years for Saturn to orbit the Sun just once, so when Saturn starts to make contact with planets in our natal chart, its effect can be felt. Its metal is lead, it is cold and dry, and its gender is male.

Saturn in Aries

Aries is not a sign that wants patience; it wants to charge ahead regardless. But when Saturn comes calling, people are forced to slow down and acquire patience and self-reliance. They are obligated to develop their own resources, thus developing strength of character.

Saturn in Taurus

These people need discipline and hard work if they are going to acquire possessions. There is a need for emotional and financial security. As Saturn has a 30-year orbit around the Sun, when people reach this age, the feeling of wanting to settle down becomes strong. This is also a time when responsibilities are placed on them.

Saturn in Gemini

This placement lends itself to a well-disciplined mind. This is useful for solving problems. Their ideas are judged on practical usefulness, and this has been proved through direct experience. People with this position like things to be in order and set down on paper. When dealing with contracts, everything has to be clear. As this air sign deals with intellectual functions, Saturn here will add stability to our thoughts. Some careers include teaching, secretarial work, physical sciences and mathematics.

Saturn in Cancer

Saturn placed in this sign can cause a restriction in emotional expression. There may be problems that start during childhood when it comes to parental relationships. These people hide their feelings from the public as they try to preserve their dignity.

Saturn in Leo

There is a need for recognition as they strive for personal control of their environment. They seek positions of power and leadership. There is a danger of becoming dictatorial or dogmatic. Defending their ego can lead to stubbornness.

Saturn in Virgo

This placement puts Saturn into an earth sign, which seems to complement each other. Saturn, with its self-discipline, placed in Virgo—concerned with accuracy, precision and efficiency—creates hardworking individuals. Their discipline can lead them to produce work of a high standard. Should someone be in a position of authority, they will expect the same standards from their employees.

Saturn in Libra

Here, cooperation is necessary in relationships, but must be enduring if they are going to be effective. Of course, this is only possible if all parties are dealt with fairly and justly, and rules of behaviour and commitment must be adhered to. This behaviour pattern grows from the understanding that human relationships entail mutual commitment. Some likely professions are lawyers, judges or mediators.

Saturn in Scorpio

People with this placement show a serious emotional intensity. As far as relationships are concerned, this can lead to great loyalty—depending on Saturn's house placement, particularly if placed in the first house. The downside here, though, is they can be too hard on themselves. They are perfectionists in their work, trying to improve the status quo.

Saturn in Sagittarius

The seriousness continues here, but this time it is linked to people's philosophical and religious beliefs. They can be someone who will stick doggedly to a traditional belief system or show the complete opposite by being an atheist. There is a depth of consideration, and this can be put to practical use. They may seek leadership in religion, law or higher education.

Saturn in Capricorn

Here, Saturn is in the first sign that it rules—the sign of the mountain goat, steadfast and secure. They seek endeavours that have a practical use. They wish to find themselves in a position of authority but can equally accept orders from others. Provided Saturn is well-aspected, there will be honesty and integrity in business and professional dealings.

Saturn in Aquarius

This is the second sign Saturn rules. Uranus was allocated to Aquarius when discovered, but Saturn has always been the traditional ruler, and both need to be taken into account. This may seem confusing, as both planets are at the opposite end of the scale: Uranus, with its carefree, anything-goes attitude; and Saturn, with its restrictions and discipline. Put this together, and you might feel chaos would ensue. However, what you get is freedom with structure. What these people want is the security (Saturn) of home, work and relationships, with the freedom (Uranus) of not being tied down. So, they can pack a bag and take off on a trip, knowing that their home and work are there to come back to. They will put their work ethics into some form of humanitarian cause. They will be loyal and responsible in group activities and to friends.

Saturn in Pisces

This can be difficult. Here you have a solid, stable and restrictive planet placed in Pisces—a sign that can be confusing. Pisces, with two fish swimming in opposite directions, is everything that Saturn is not. This is said to be a karmic planet in a karmic sign. Here, problems can arise that are difficult or impossible to diagnose, as they might have their roots in a past life. If there is anything we have brought back with us to resolve, Saturn will be aspecting the South Node in our charts. It can cause all sorts of anxieties, and people find it difficult to live in the present. They have the ability to create problems that don't really exist in this lifetime. The good side to this placement is that there is a great deal of emotional understanding and a willingness to work hard for those less fortunate than themselves.

Chapter 6
The Signs

I shall now go through the signs of the zodiac, their elements and mode of behaviour, but to start off, let's have a light-hearted look at how they respond to a given situation.

The Bus Stop

There are twelve people standing at a bus stop. Each is a different sign of the zodiac. The bus is late, and this is how they react:

(♈) Aries starts running to work.
(♉) Taurus knows the bus will come and is patient.
(♊) Gemini starts talking to everyone.
(♋) Cancer gets upset and takes it all personally.
(♌) Leo entertains everyone.
(♍) Virgo starts to worry about his meetings being late.
(♎) Libra tries to pacify Virgo.
(♏) Scorpio is planning what to do to the driver.
(♐) Sagittarius is probably cycling.

(♑) Capricorn knew all along the bus would be late.
(♒) Aquarius is redesigning the city's transport system.
(♓) Pisces hasn't noticed.
– *Anon.*

The sign are split up into two groups:
1. 3x4 =12 The Elements
2. 4x3 =12 The Modes of Expression

Before we start looking into the signs more deeply, I will just explain the elements and modes. First, the elements. All the signs are split into Fire, Earth, Air and Water, and stay in that order around a chart.

Fire

People born under the signs of Aries, Leo and Sagittarius seek to display leadership in some way.

> Aries is about decisiveness and spearheading new efforts.
> Leo possesses the managerial capacity and can be a dramatic figure in any organisation.
> Sagittarius has the ability for spiritual and philosophic leadership.

Earth

These come with the attributes of practicality. These signs can produce a skill in using and managing material and financial resources.

Taurus likes to accumulate material resources.
Virgo is very precise.
Capricorn wants to organise.

Air

The three Air signs are:

> Gemini—The ability to acquire and utilise factual information.
> Libra—Qualities manifested as the ability to weigh and balance, making just comparisons.
> Aquarius—Intuitive grasp of universal principles.

Water

These signs add an emotional element to any planet that falls in the following signs:

> Cancer—Strong feelings about home and family.
> Scorpio—Concern with the deeper mysteries of life.
> Pisces—Unconscious telepathic communication with others, including a sympathetic awareness of the environment.

Now we come to the modes of expression. There are broken down into Cardinal, Fixed and Mutable.

Cardinal signs are action signs. Each group has one sign from each element. The easiest way to explain this is as follows:

> Aries (Fire): I want action, and I want it now.
> Cancer (Water): I want action, but how does everyone feel about it?

Libra (Air): I want action, but is it fair?
Capricorn (Earth): I want action, so let's get organised.

Fixed signs are Taurus, Leo, Scorpio and Aquarius. People born under these signs achieve results through persistence and determination. Success comes over a sustained period of time, with stubbornness and rigidity added to the mix.

Mutable signs are also known as double-bodied. These signs are able to adapt to changing circumstances.
Gemini—The twins.
Virgo—The original portrayal is a winged woman.
Sagittarius—Half man, half horse.
Pisces—Two fish swimming in opposite directions.

The signs are broken down further into male and female:

Male: Aries, Gemini, Leo, Libra, Sagittarius and Aquarius.
Female: Taurus, Cancer, Virgo, Scorpio, Capricorn and Pisces.

So, all the Fire and Air signs are male, and the Earth and Water signs are female.

Now, we take a deeper look into each sign.

Aries (♈) Fire, Male, Cardinal, Hot and dry
Key Phrase: 'I Am'

The first sign of the zodiac starts at the Spring Equinox, around the 21st of March—the start of the astrological year. This is a time of new life. Spring has arrived, and the earth is waking up after the long winter months. Aries is a baby—full of energy. Ruled by Mars, this fiery sign initiates new activities but may not stay around long enough to see them completed, or until the novelty wears off. There is a psychological drive to prove themselves through action. Anyone with Mars near the Ascendant, or with an Aries Ascendant, is likely to have red hair. They can achieve a lot in life if they can learn to think before they act. Difficulties can arise because of their impulsive nature. The more highly evolved Aries types possess great willpower, spiritual self-confidence and regenerative ability, due to the Sun's exaltation in this sign. Medically, Aries rules the head—and they do go into things headfirst. Some may remember the song by Cat Stevens, 'Matthew and Son'. This is a very good example of how this sign works.

Taurus (♉) Earth, Female, Fixed, Cold and dry
Key Phrase: 'I Have'

Taurus is ruled by Venus. This sign is born to achieve mastery over physical matter. They strive for spiritual truth by working with the practical aspects of life. This sign is fond of the good things in life. They enjoy good food and have a high appreciation of beauty, especially that which appeals to the sense of touch. As Taurus is a fixed earth sign, this beauty extends to the Earth itself. Taureans make good gardeners. The Moon is exalted in Taurus, and, should it be placed there, creating something of beauty with the Earth will bring enormous emotional satisfaction. In medical astrology,

Taurus rules the throat. Now, thinking back to the planets in the chapter on the ages—do you remember how Uranus behaves? There may be something odd or different about their voice, or perhaps their singing. The best way to explain this, of course, is Julie Andrews with 'The Lonely Goatherd' from 'The Sound of Music'. As she has Uranus in Taurus, it was this configuration that gave her a five-octave range, which she put to good use during her career. Taurus likes to accumulate possessions, and this can lead to hoarding.

Gemini (♊) Male, Air, Hot and Moist, Mutable
Key Phrase: 'I Think'

This intellectual Air sign, ruled by Mercury, gives the ability to think swiftly. If ever there was a sign that epitomised multi-tasking, it's this one. Gemini, the sign of the twins, can cope with more than one activity at the same time. Verbal communication is very important and acts as an anchoring or safety device as they jump from one thing to another.

Medically, Gemini rules the hands and arms, as well as the nerves, which gives a talent for making things. They experience a great deal of pleasure bringing their ideas into form—and their ideas are plentiful. Their creations can be artistic or academic. They need to work to acquire calmness of mind as well as of body. They can be prone to nervous tension if there is not enough mental stimulation. Gemini is a very social sign. They can enjoy great popularity because of their witty conversation, mental agility and social ability. They dislike being bound to one place or person. They are fond of travel, and there is a touch of the child with this sign. Refusing to grow old, Gemini delights in tricks, puzzles and is the ever-practical joker.

Cancer (♋) Female, Water, Cold and Moist, Cardinal
Key Phrase: 'I Feel'

This cardinal water sign is about action, but there will always be an element of feeling. This sign favours women more than men and is the strongest of the water signs, linked to care for the home and family. The crab shell—Cancer's symbol—represents the armour which hides extreme sensitivity, shyness and vulnerability. When hurt emotionally, it's the shell they hide in to seek solitude. Cancer is ruled by the Moon; its waxing and waning cycles are seen in the Cancer personality. There can be a great fluctuation in moods—one moment they can be outgoing, the next melancholic.

The house that has Cancer on the cusp is where a great deal of emotion expression is played out. If on the 10th house cusp of career, people will enter a caring profession. Nursing comes to mind.

Leo (♌) Male, Fire, Hot and Dry, Fixed
Key Phrase: 'I Will'

Leo the Lion—the head of the pride. And there is a great deal of pride displayed here. Ruled by the Sun, Leos want to shine in whatever they do. The house that has Leo on the cusp is where this will manifest. They possess a sense of integrity and assume others do too. They can be confident, frank and outspoken. Should Leo be in a position of authority and responsibility, they will leave no stone unturned in order to justify the confidence placed in them. Leos function well in management, enjoying the responsibilities they hold. Being a fixed sign, they will push steadfastly on until they achieve what they want. Leo is not a sign that functions behind the scenes—they want to be seen and noticed. For this reason, they can make good actors. The lion denotes power, majesty and dignity; they express pride in every movement, especially if Leo is on the cusp of the first house. It is quite noticeable when they stand up—they always straighten their back before they start walking, and the head is held high. Medically, Leo rules the heart. Relationships are also a matter of pride, and serious heartache can result should a relationship collapse. Many public figures have the Sun in Leo: Barak Obama, Amelia Earhart—who flew solo over the Atlantic in May 1932—and tennis player Roger Federer. These people have displayed commitment, courage and sportsmanship in their tasks.

Virgo (♍) Female, Cold and Dry, Earth, Mutable
Key Phrase: 'I Analyse'

This is the sign that has *efficiency* written all over it. Virgos will always try to bring order out of confusion. They are very meticulous in their work, paying a great deal of attention to detail. They make good accountants, bookkeepers and secretaries. Medically, Virgo rules the stomach, and stress or nervousness can often lead to stomach upsets. Virgo is also strongly connected to health in general, and they can spend their money on health issues. They are always mindful of their own fitness. As an earth sign, Virgo enjoys good food and is fond of comfort and quality clothing. The fashion industry is one area where they may seek employment. They dislike shoddy workmanship. This a sign that seeks perfection, which is particularly evident in relationships. They are always looking for the perfect partner. As mentioned, Virgo's key phrase is 'I analyse', and this is no exaggeration. They will analyse everything to the point of talking themselves out of progress. If the Moon is in Virgo, it's their emotions that come under the microscope, which can block spontaneity. By the time they arrive at a decision, the opportunity may have passed. Mercury, the ruler of Virgo, behaves very differently here than in Gemini. Gone is the flitting about from one thing to another—as the mind concentrates on the task at hand. Virgo can be critical, as not everyone they come into contact with will have the same standards. Their leisure activities may include health clubs, yoga, walking and indoor pursuits such as arts and crafts, carpentry or wood carving.

Libra (♎) Male, Hot and Moist. Cardinal, Air
Key Phrase: 'I Balance'

This sign, ruled by Venus, brings charm and grace in expression. Librans seek approval from others and often possess a natural beauty and elegance. Being the sign of the scales, Libra is often cited as being the most balanced sign of the zodiac—but this is not always the case. Libras can swing from one end of the scale to the other or just sit on the fence. Relationships are important to them—they require harmony in their lives for their well-being and may go to great length to achieve it. Often, they sacrifice their own needs to accommodate others, yet beneath that soft exterior lies a tough character.

This sign is excellent in the field of negotiation. A tactful and diplomatic personality, Libra will smooth matters down and find middle ground. There is a strong sense of justice. They are anything but lazy, owing to the influence of Saturn. Since Libra is a cardinal sign, they are connected with the present and will initiate activities—but they will seek the cooperation of others rather than continuing alone. Subjects like psychology and human relationships are of deep interest to them. They make good counsellors and often seek to help people with their problems, frequently playing the role of the peacemaker. They rarely express anger, but when they do, it can feel like a tornado has swept through the room—they leave nothing unsaid. Like a tornado, their anger is soon gone, leaving them shaken.

Scorpio (♏) Female, Cold and Dry, Fixed, Water
Key Phrase: 'Regeneration'

Scorpio, the third of the water signs, is fixed in its nature. This sign always seems to get bad press because of the inevitable sting in the tail. It doesn't bode well to make an enemy of this sign—Scorpio never forgets a hurt. It's a sign that, when hurt, rises from the ashes stronger than before. There is a bird related to this sign: 'The Phoenix'. Scorpio has two rulers: Mars and Pluto. It's Pluto that gives the regenerative powers to the sign. Scorpios are very good at keeping their emotions firmly under wraps and give the impression they are not affected by emotional upset—but feelings run deep with this sign. Scorpio is likened to icebergs: most of the ice is beneath the surface. Scorpios make good investigators; they like to get to the root of a problem before sorting it out. There is no point in trying to fix something if it can return later. They make good detectives, scientists, doctors or private investigators. As far as interests are concerned, they like to delve into the world of mysticism, but also enjoy sports—especially those leaning towards the dangerous side, due to the Mars connection. Because of their fixed mode of expression, Scorpios do not like change. Personal exposure is also hard for them to deal with. Like Pluto, they prefer to hide behind a mask. In general, they are robust and strong built, and are noted for their keenly penetrating eyes and strong aura of personal mystique and magnetism. Their intuition is usually well–developed, as they seem to penetrate the inner thoughts of others.

Sagittarius (♐) Male, Mutable, Hot and Dry, Fire
Key Phrase: 'I See'

Sagittarians are born under the sign of honesty and straightforwardness and are represented by the arrow that flies swiftly to its goal. They love liberty and freedom. Energetic and naturally outgoing, they achieve their goals through the power of positive thinking. As a rule, women with this sign are not fond of domestic tasks and tend to be very independent. Sagittarians have the ability to see the future by understanding current trends of thought, and on occasion, their insights boarder on prophecy. They do not have a subtle approach to life and can jump to conclusions. Sagittarius is ruled by the planet Jupiter and is a mutable sign—the third of the double-bodied signs, half man and half horse. For some, having Sagittarius on the 10th house cusp of career can lead to working with horses. They are fond of wide open spaces and travel, which adds to their learning and philosophy of life. While this can be enriching, it can also be impractical—they lean towards ideas rather than application. When working through problems, they can come up with unconventional ideas that actually work. Sagittarians can be the eternal student, always asking the big questions and seeking the meaning of life. Their leisure activities range from sports, hiking, camping and mountain biking to horse riding. In terms of study, subjects like languages, religions or philosophy may be of particular interest.

Capricorn (♑) Earth, Female, Cardinal, Cold and Dry

Key Phrase: 'Ambition'

The sure-footed mountain goat, intent on climbing the ladder of success—Capricorns are born with the feeling that they must develop into something. The last of the cardinal signs is about action with organisation. Their intuition is excellent, and they use it to achieve personal independence and economic security. As Capricorn is an earth sign, everything has to be sensible. They are never deterred by obstacles that stand in the way of their climb to the top. There can be an extreme capacity for hard work, knowing that this will lead to material security—and they will work and plan for it. They are very good at problem-solving and make good troubleshooters. Some of the careers Capricorns might pursue include chief executive officer, civil servant, pensions consultant, politician, bank manager or teacher. As Capricorn is medically linked to the skeletal system, chiropractor, orthopaedic surgeon, osteopath and dentists are other possibilities. Given that Capricorns like structure, surveyor, builder or geologist are also viable career options. When they get time off, Capricorn will take to the hills for walking or climbing, as they feel at home in that environment. Their hobbies can include yoga, golf, genealogy, gardening, pottery and DIY. Saturn is the ruler of this sign, and there may be a tendency to be melancholic and, at times, lonely. They have sensitive personalities and want to be appreciated.

Aquarius (♒) Male, Fixed, Hot and Moist,
Key Phrase: 'Freedom and Humanitarianism'

For those born under this sign of brotherhood and fraternity, their symbol is the Water Bearer, who spills out to mankind the life force of spiritual energy. You could be forgiven for thinking Aquarius is a water sign, but its element is actually Air. Aquarius is a fixed sign, and being an air sign, can display fixed ideas—it's hard to change their minds. Uranus is one of its rulers, which can bring eccentricity to their temperament. They can be determined and stubborn. They sometimes feel others are unable to understand their ideas, due to Uranus always being one step ahead. Friends are very important to them. They act as an equal among equals but do not depend on their environment for security; they derive it from being in the company of others. The other ruler of Aquarius is Saturn. Should Saturn fall in Aquarius, there is the ability to quiet the mind and steady the attention—both necessary for the development of the Uranian intuitive faculties. Wherever Saturn falls in the chart, if there is any contact with the Sun or any planet in Aquarius, this development can occur. There can be a rebellious side to this sign—a genius and a misfit, all at the same time. They are strongly motivated by a social conscience. They understand what the world will need many years down the line and can initiate change now. Without Aquarius, there would be no revolution. There is a love of freedom here, especially in wide open spaces. Interests can include hiking or long walks, and if there is a hill to be climbed, they will climb it.

Pisces (♓) Female, Water, Cold and Moist, Mutable
Key Phrase: 'Compassion'

We have reached the last sign of the zodiac: Pisces. This mutable water sign, with its two fishes swimming in opposite directions, perfectly describes the confusion sometimes suffered by this sign. The mind flows where it will; it can enter the realms of the mystical and transcend. Pisces finds the harsh realities of life hard to cope with and often find themselves acting like a martyr. They are caring and compassionate but may find it hard to stop giving and doing everything for someone else. Emotions underpin everything in life. Sometimes, they have difficulty knowing what they feel, as they have the ability to pick up the emotions of everyone they come into contact with. Their talents stem from anything artistic—acting, dancing, fantasy writing—anything that helps them escape the norm. Pisces also enjoys the mystical side of life, so priest, healer, tarot reader or astrologer are all possibilities. They dislike detail, time constraints, reality and telling the truth if it is going to hurt someone. They can go through life wearing rose-coloured glasses—especially when it comes to relationships. They are blind to the defects in those they love and trust. Pisces is ruled by Jupiter and Neptune—Jupiter with its expansive qualities, and Neptune ruling the realms of the sea. It is easy to understand how Pisces reacts to the outside world and swims in the expansive oceans of life.

The Astrologer's Prayer

♈ **Teach me how to be**
          and be aware ♎
♉ **Teach how to have**

        and how to share ♏
♊ Teach me to understand
        as well as to know ♐
♋ Teach me how to root
        and how to grow ♑
♌ Teach me to love
        and to be free ♒
♍ To be of service
        and come to thee ♓

Rev Pamela Crane, DFAstrolS, DMS Astrol (Hons)

Chapter 7:
Planetary Conditions

Now that we have looked at the planets and signs, it is time to see how the planets function in different signs. In the graph below, you will see that there are four different placements for this to materialise: rulership, detriment, exaltation and fall. I will be using the glyphs to show this.

Sign	Rulership	Detriment	Exaltation	Fall
♈	♂	♀	☉	♄
♉	♀	♂	☽	♅
♊	☿	♃	-	-
♋	☽	♄	♃	♂
♌	☉	♄	-	-
♍	☿	♃♆	☿	♀
♎	♀	♂	♄	☉
♏	♂♇	♀	♅	☽
♐	♃	☿	-	-
♑	♄	☽	♂	♃
♒	♄♅	☉	-	-
♓	♃♆	☿	♀	☿

Rulership

Planets that fall in the sign of their rulership want to shine in whatever path they have chosen.

Detriment

A detrimented sign is always opposite the sign of rulership. Planets falling in this condition function at a grassroots level; i.e. the Sun in Aquarius could mean a community social worker.

Exaltation

Someone powerful, but not in a powerful place. Focus on excess.

Fall

A feeling that one has slipped or lost something. Trying to connect to something. Looking to gain power. Jupiter in Capricorn is aware of a lack of excess.

To explain this better, if you go back to Chapter Two and look at the charts of Edward VIII and George VI, you will notice that Jupiter in the chart of Edward VIII is in the sign of Gemini—its detriment. It also has contact with Saturn, ruler of his first house, the Ascendant, and Jupiter rules his 10th house of career. Jupiter is weakened by this placement, obstructed by Saturn (the chart ruler), and next to Neptune, adding confusion to his state of mind. Gemini rules the mind and thinking. This, of course, does not bode well for his career—and the rest is history.

If you look at the chart of George VI, you will find Jupiter is placed in the 10th house of career, in the sign of Leo. Jupiter is the planet linked to a monarch. Leo, the Lion, is the king of the jungle. Although Jupiter does not appear in the sign of its rulership or exaltation, it does function very well in any of the fire signs, so this placement is far stronger. The Moon is in its fall, and Venus is in its detriment—which rules the chart. Also, Venus is close to Saturn, placing restrictions on him. He also wanted to break free, as Uranus is in the first house. Uranus is in the sign of its exaltation: someone powerful, but not in a powerful place. Even a king can't have everything his own way. Everyone knew how he struggled with his position, but still he served his country—especially through the dark days of World War II.

If you go back to the *Astrologer's Prayer,* you will see the prayer is written in six blocks of two.

Each block has two signs attached; these signs are polar opposites.

Chapter 8
The Houses

There are twelve houses that make up a chart. Sometimes there will be one sign on the cusp of each house, but in other cases, one or more signs may occupy a single house. This depends on the house system being used. The first six houses relate to your personality and your inner world; the last six reflect how you relate to the outside world and your interactions with others. One thing worth mentioning is that not all houses have planets in them. This often causes concern. Some houses may have several planets. In such situations, any planet in one house will rule another. Now, the houses become linked. For example, the ruler of the second house might be placed in the 9th. The second house deals with how you earn your money. If its ruler is placed in the 9th, this could manifest in teaching, as a travel agent, or even a role in the church.

1st House

This house is also known as the Ascendant. It's for this reason that the time of birth is required. With the correct time, a sign will be placed on the left side of the chart. This is the window that provides you with your view of the world—who you are and how you meet life. This sign is how you grow into your Sun sign, and it also influences your physical appearance. Here are some examples of how a rising sign can integrate with the Sun sign:

Someone with the Sun in Aries and Virgo on the Ascendant could discover that the ability to initiate projects (Aries) will require an ability to approach things in a focused and precise manner (Virgo). The Sun in Pisces with Libra on the Ascendant may find the path of healing and serving others (Pisces) through the importance of one-to-one relationships or artistic talents (Libra).

2nd House

With the 1st house, our individual identity has now manifested, and our approach to life has been defined. The task now is further elaboration—producing a more solid sense of who we are. We need some idea of what we possess and what we can call our own. This doesn't only relate to our physical possessions. What we own can also be what we value, or how we earn a living, so we can structure our lives. The sign on the cusp of the 2nd house will describe how we go about maintaining our security. Different things represent security to different people. For instance, if Gemini is ruling the 2nd house and Mercury is in the 2nd, then acquiring knowledge can make this person feel safe. Pisces here could derive their security from a spiritual philosophy, music or art. If something makes you feel safe and secure, then naturally we will want to acquire it. Another area that can bring about security is the talents you possess. A talent you develop can lead to a way of earning a living. Should this house be empty, look to the house where the ruler is located—this can show where a living can be earned. For example, the ruler of the

2nd house in the 5th could suggest a profession in arts and crafts or as an estate agent. We tend to base our whole life on what we value and strive to gain, so this house is crucial. As we grow, we shape our entire existence around these criteria. When our values change, our whole life focus can shift dramatically. One way this can occur is when a planet makes its way into the 2nd house. The slower the planet, the more dramatic the effect. Alternatively, the ruler may be aspected from somewhere else in the chart. Suddenly, you start to see things differently. What you once went along with may begin to grate on your nerves—until you can no longer take it and decide to do something about it.

3rd House

The sign on the cusp of the 3rd house reveals the mode in which we communicate with others and how we make sense of the world around us. Any planets placed here will modify this expression. It can also influence what we choose to do in our career. This house also brings us into contact with early relationships—the first being siblings and school friends. Planets placed here can indicate the bond between us and a sibling. The 3rd house reflects our early school experiences. School gives us the opportunity to see what we are like with people outside our family unit and to compare what our parents have told us with what others have to say. We also learn as much from our peers as we do from our teachers. Throughout childhood, we assimilate more and more information, which ultimately forms a code of practical rules and contributes to who we are. We need some idea of what we possess and what we can call our own—and this doesn't only relate to our physical possessions. What we own can also refer to what we value or how we earn a living, which helps us structure our lives. The sign on the cusp of the 2nd house will describe how we go about maintaining our security. Different things represent security to different people. For instance, if Gemini rules the 2nd house and Mercury is in the 2nd, then acquiring knowledge can make this person feel safe. Pisces here could derive their security from a spiritual philosophy, music or art. If something makes you feel safe and secure, then naturally, you will want to acquire it. Another area that can bring about security is the talents you possess. A talent you develop can lead to a way of earning a living. Should this house be empty, look to the house where the ruler is located—this can show where a living can be earned. For example, if the ruler of the 2nd is in the 5th, this might indicate a career in arts and crafts or as an estate agent. We tend to base our whole lives on what we value and on the pursuit of gain. Therefore, this house is crucial. As we grow, we build our entire existence around these criteria. When our values change, our whole life focus can shift dramatically. One way this shift can occur is when a planet makes its way into the second house. The slower the planet, the more dramatic the effect. Alternatively, the ruler may be aspected from somewhere else in the chart. Suddenly, you begin to see things differently. What you once went along with may begin to grate on your nerves—and will keep doing so until you can no longer tolerate it and decide to do something about it.

3rd House

The sign on the cusp of the third house is the mode in which we communicate with others, and how we make sense of the world around us. Any planets placed here will modify this action. It can also aid what we will do with regards to a career. This house also brings us into contact with early relationships, the first being siblings and school friends. Planets placed here denote the bond between us and a sibling. The third house shows something about our early school days and experiences there. School gives us a chance to see what we are like with people outside the family unit and to compare what our parents have told us with what others have to say. We also learn as much from our piers as we do from our teachers. Throughout childhood we assimilate more and more information which, in the end, forms a code of practical rules and truths, by which we give order and meaning to life. In mythology, Mercury has an affiliation with the 3rd house. He was in charge of distributing information, so this house draws connections between fields of study or branches of knowledge. Planets placed in this house can influence how we deal with third–house matters. Saturn, for instance, can cause problems with study—there may be a block in retaining knowledge, or a real effort put into learning. Uranus can bring very odd ideas and revolutionary thinking, which may border on genius. Mars placed here can mean knowledge is power, but there may be sibling rivalry, and this house can become a battleground. Venus can bring about harmonious relationships with siblings and peers. Knowledge may include the arts and music. Neptune may lead to a dreamy existence, with a deep interest in spiritual subjects. However, powers of concentration may be poor. The 3rd house introduces us to how we interact with others. The sign on its cusp will determine how we approach this essential function.

4th House

We have now arrived at the 2nd of the angular houses. The 4th house cusp and the sign placed there shows how we will experience home life. There has been a great deal of discussion on which parent is linked to this house. A number of astrologers lean towards the mother, as she is the focus of any baby's attention, but there is also a constructive argument for the father to rule the 4th, as children inherit their father's surname. The ancient astrologers placed the father here. Now we are finding our own identity and what is important to us, we have to integrate this into family life. The sign on the cusp of the 4th will show how this area plays out. Sagittarius can mean a large house, father is likely to be jovial character. Aquarius could mean a great deal of moving about and upheaval, also, in the end, we may find we are happier if we live alone and have our freedom. Also, home life can be unusual. It can be the place for study of new age or alternative subjects, astrology comes to mind. Any water sign placed here can produce a loving environment, home life can be an emotional one. Each of us sees our home life through the sign on the cusp of the 4th house, so a large family under one roof will see it from a different perspective, it's this early view that gives us our childhood experience of home, and what we will seek to repeat when we have our own. The sign on the cusp of the 4th also shows how we end things, this will be modified by planets placed there. Venus ends things neatly and fairly, Saturn may prolong or begrudge an ending. The Moon or Neptune often slip away quietly, but Mars or Uranus will go out with a bang. For those who are interested, meditation or self-reflection can help bring forth issues to the surface so we can process them. Like our past, the 4th house always catches up with us.

5th House

We have now arrived at the 5th house. The 4th house is where we discover our identity, but in the 5th others will see where our interests lie and what we do for fun and relaxation. The 5th house is linked to creative expression, and this may have a link or end up being a profession, depending where the ruler is placed. The sign on the cusp will also modify this. Creativity, fun and hobbies, may not always be light hearted. Having Saturn or Capricorn on the cusp can lead to activities that not everyone would get enjoyment from. Place Gemini on the cusp and Saturn in the 5th, and one activity could be setting crosswords. Aquarius there could be scientific, while Cancer could set up some caring facility, or along with Taurus may get a great deal of pleasure from cooking. The 5th house can also be described as the house of the inner child. This is the part of us that loves to play and stays eternally young. Inside all of us is a spontaneous natural child, who craves to be loved for their own specialness and uniqueness. Sometimes as children, this part of us is sometimes squashed, as we are expected to live up to our parents' expectations rather than being allowed to be ourselves. This continues through the school years, as we battle through study and exams, trying to fit into what the system expects of us, gradually losing faith in our own individuality and end up as the adapted child. As the 5th house is about children, it will eventually become the house of our children, as some of the creative ability we have can pass down to the next generation. If our childhood talents and creativity never unfold, we can try and force this onto our children, but each chart is individual to its owner, and the creativity they have may be very different from our own. On some occasions, how or what we create can lead to a career. In the 5th house, we create for ourselves, as we take joy in doing so, but mainly because it is an inherent part of human nature.

6th House

Now that we have explored the creative side to our nature, the sixth house shows how we bring order and routine to our lives by imposing a little discipline. Here, we have to realise that to get through everyday life, work is required to keep body and soul together. It is this house that makes us come down to reality and keep a pattern so we can function. The sign on the cusp will show how you approach work; any planets in the 6th will, of course, modify this. The 6th has concerns for craftsmanship and technical proficiency and applies to health issues as well as work. Many are especially interested in health and fitness, but some can be obsessive about this, leaving little time for anything else. However, many excellent healers have a 6th house emphasis, which can be associated with traditional medicine, homeopathy, and herbalism. Our well-being also lies in another area which may sound insignificant, but this can have a bearing on our well-being. Pets are assigned to the 6th house. Some are profoundly affected by their experience of looking after an animal. For those who find themselves alone after years of marriage, a new lease of life will be given when a four-footed friend moves in. The company they provide, in turn, has health benefits for the owner. Through sixth issues, we refine and perfect ourselves and become a better channel for being who we are. We could be the most inspired artist (5th house), but unless we can learn the tools of the craft (6th), we won't be able to realise our possibilities. Techniques is the liberation of the imagination.

7th House

The 6th house is the last of what is known as the personal houses and represents the refinement of the individual personality through work, service, attention to everyday life and the physical body. By the end of the 6th house, we have grown as separate from one another as life will allow, and we have a new lesson to learn. Nothing exists in isolation. When we arrive at the 7th house, the western point in a chart, we find ourselves looking back at the point where it all began. The 1st house is self-awareness; the 7th house is awareness of others. Planets placed here can affect our reactions to relationships. Mars can see you rushing in headfirst, love at first sight, or where your battleground can be. Jupiter can mean a number of relationships. Neptune will have on a pair of rose-coloured glasses. The 7th house is not only for partnerships; it's everyone we come into contact with, and the planets placed there can have an effect on others. Mars there can stir everyone into action; Saturn may bring out the teacher or mentor. Many people involved in the caring professions have an emphasis on the 7th.

8th House

Now that we have established our own way of maintaining our resources, we find ourselves in someone else's world with the same issue. The 8th house deals with someone else's money. This will be how our partner earns theirs—mortgages, taxes, inheritance all come under the 8th house. It also describes that which is shared and how we unite with others. Expanding on what has begun in the 7th house, the 8th is the nitty-gritty of relationships. The 8th house will see us lose our childhood and grow into adolescents, and again move into adulthood. This can lead to some degree of pain or crisis. In surviving difficult times, we emerge renewed, cleansed and wiser about ourselves and life in general. An overview is gained which allows us to see life as a journey and a process of unfoldment.

9th House

The 9th house is mainly concerned with philosophy and religion, but this may not be any traditional belief system. This is a house where you can explore many kinds of faith, or where you can formulate your own. Planets in the 9th will show how this will happen. Uranus can force you to break with tradition, but it can also show you a way to your own belief system, even if it is something completely different. Saturn here can mean sticking fast to traditional ways, or it may indicate an atheist. The 9th house is linked to travel and long-distance trips. This can be taken literally—to other lands and cultures—or more symbolically, as journeys of the mind or spirit, the broadened horizons gained from extensive reading, or insights gained through meditation. Journeys of the mind also fall into the category of higher education. Uranus, Saturn or Mercury can lead to the study of astrology, while Neptune may concentrate on music. However, Neptune here can also cause confusion on which direction to take. In the 3rd house, we are faced with what is directly in front of us; in the 9th, we get a glimpse of what is not only further away but also up and coming. Strong placements in the 9th show an unusual degree of intuition and foresight—the ability to sense the direction in which someone or something is heading.

10th House

We have now reached the highest point of the chart. The 10th house cusp, also known as the Midheaven, symbolically places any planets placed here in a position to stand out above all the others in the chart. The qualities of any sign or planet here correspond to what in us is most visible and accessible to others. At the other side of the chart, the 4th house planets show what we keep private. The 10th house planets show what we want to be admired for, looked up to, and respected for. It's through the sign and planets here that we hope to gain achievement, honour, recognition and determine what we want to be remembered for—our contribution to the world. There is a degree of ambition here; what lurks is an urge and compulsion to be esteemed and acknowledged. The 10th house also has a bearing on our careers. The house may not come to fruition until later in life. We may go through most of our working lives doing other things, which equip us with the knowledge and confidence to eventually take on what will be ours,—and this can take many years. Saturn in the 10th may end up teaching. Uranus could become connected to IT, electrics or invention, though this may manifest only after many years of being unsettled in a conventional role. Mars could bring military service or sports; Venus and Neptune, the arts. The 10th house also shows the relationship with our mother. This is modified by the planets placed here. At the start of life, she is the whole world to us. How we bond with her will be reflected later in life in how we relate to the outside world in general. We have come a long way from the first house to the 10th. In the 1st, we were not even aware of who we were; by the time the 10th house is reached, we have developed sufficiently and have a good sense of who we are and how to recognise it.

11th House

This house shows where we find our identity in a group situation or with friends. The sign on the cusp will lead us to a group where we feel we belong. Opposite the 5th house, we will draw friends and join group situations where we feel we can enhance our creativity—also giving us a better sense of who we are. Planets found in the 11th will modify the groups we could be found joining: Neptune—local spiritual or music groups; Uranus—astrology groups or IT clubs; Mercury—a book club or writing group; Mars—a local sports group or groups who put on displays of battles. The sign on the cusp shows what you are looking for in a friend or group. Aries is all about action; Cancer, more homely and caring associations; Pisces, artistic, musical and spiritual; Taurus, down-to-earth and practical groups and friends that are into gardening. Friends, as mentioned earlier, fit into the 11th house. The ideal here is becoming greater than we already are. People are linked together through friendships. Personal boundaries are expanded, and both the needs and resources of others become interwoven with our ideas and interests. Likewise, we are broadened by what they have to share. Again, as with the group situation, any planets in the 11th will draw us to people with these qualities. However, these same placements may also show these qualities in ourselves that we disown, project outwardly and most externally through friends. If a man with Mars in the 11th has not developed his own Mars side and lacks that certain 'get up and go', his friends will provide the energy.

12th House

We arrive at the 12th house. There is a feeling that the individual's ego needs to let go, and we need to unite with something that is greater than ourselves. This doesn't mean via the mind or intellect, but with our heart and soul. Planets placed here can show difficulties and old trouble spots. A well-placed Mars here can show courage, strength and forthrightness have already been learnt and will sustain the native through challenging times—emerging just when they are needed. The 12th house is also linked to confinement: hospitals, prisons and any institution which removes people from their everyday environment. It is said to be the house of secret enemies. To a degree, this is true, but we can also be our own worst enemy because of the difficulty of integrating the planets placed here into everyday life. Some with the Sun placed here can spend a lifetime behind the scenes, working quietly in the background. Uranus may want to settle down with a partner but scupper their own chances to do so, as Uranus always wants to break free.

Chapter 9
The Nodes of the Moon

The Nodes of the Moon have a bearing on our spiritual path for this lifetime. They are not physical bodies in space, but mathematical points. They do not emit light or give out the energy from the signs they are in, nor do they change or adjust how the sign is experienced. However, they do produce a pure meaning of the sign they are located in. The two Nodes are the North Node (☊) and the South Node (☋)—what the ancient astrologers called *Caput Draconis* (Dragon's Head) and *Cauda Draconis* (Dragon's Tail). The Nodes of the Moon are always opposite each other. In a chart, the planets move in an anticlockwise direction, but the Nodes moves clockwise. When the Sun and Moon are close to either the North or South Node, a solar eclipse will occur. Similarly, when the Moon is close to one node and the Sun is opposite the Moon and near the opposite node, a lunar eclipse will be taking place. When a planet comes into contact with the Nodes, it can trigger the meaning of the Node and the spiritual path you are on. The faster planets may not be felt so profoundly, but the slower planets will have a deeper impact. First of all, we must understand the signs the Nodes are in and the houses they fall in. The house will direct you to an area of life that needs attention. The South Node (☋) is where we are coming from. The sign you find it in is where you are most comfortable. Subconsciously, you retreat to the South Node because it feels safe. When the going gets tough, the tough get going—'backwards'. The South Node is connected to past life experiences. Planets in contact with it show issues you carried with you into this lifetime—issues you will need to address at some point. As a practicing astrologer, I soon found that the problems clients asked me to help with often had their roots in a past life. It is not something we think about daily, but the reality is that these hidden dynamics affect the way we behave and react to certain situations. These problems can become very severe—outside agencies such as the health service, police and local authorities may become involved, unaware of the deeper root of the issue. There is a book by American astrologer Steven Forrest called 'Yesterday's Sky'—a very good read on astrology and reincarnation.

The North Node (☊) represents where we are heading in this lifetime. It shows the task at hand—and for many, it won't be easy. You are out of your comfort zone here, and there will be times when you wish you could turn the clock back to how things were, whether in relationships, career or home life. The example I shall be dealing with is my own (Fig 10).

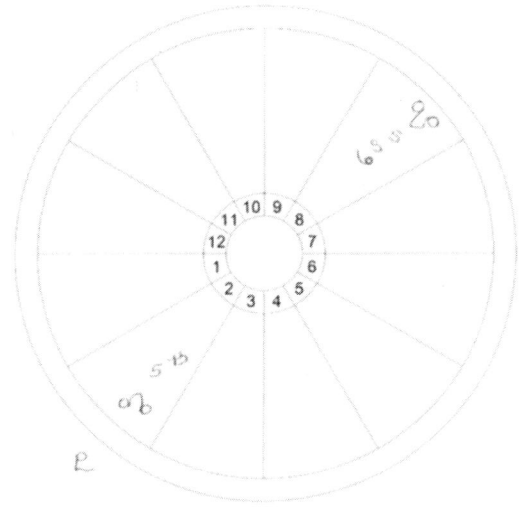

Fig 10

I have the South Node (☋) in Cancer in the 8th house, and the North Node (☊) in Capricorn in the 2nd house. Looking at the chapter on the signs and houses, you find Cancer is about home, family, roots and emotional and financial security—this being given from others, as the 8th deals with the finances of a significant other. The North Node is in

Capricorn. This is about developing your own security, and to do this, you need to take on the responsibility and develop it. The North Node doesn't come easily. In this case, what it meant was that, at some point, I would take the plunge and be single again. What I didn't expect is that I would be the one to leave the marriage, move to the other end of the country, and start afresh. Before this happened, I was watching Pluto getting closer to the North Node and wondering what it meant. I soon found out. I decided not to fight it—just to go with the flow. It was a few years before I finally left, but Pluto had crossed my North Node and done its job. I understood what was needed. Life has worked out very well. I sometimes wonder what would have happened if I had stayed. Being an astrologer helped—I had something to show me the way. It's nonetheless frightening. There were moments when I wondered if I was doing the right thing, but it all worked out very well. It must be a lonely experience for those who have to go through something like this—if they don't know what their chart is doing, or even realise they have one.

Part 3

Chapter 10
An Astrological Act of Remembrance

As mentioned earlier, when people think of astrology, they mainly focus on the signs and planets—and to a certain degree, that is true. The ancient astrologers were also aware that there were other factors at work as well. These factors are documented in ancient texts but are largely forgotten today. Medieval astrology incorporates these factors, which add greater depth to a reading. There are many departments in astrology: natal, dealing with birth charts; medical; financial; electional astrology (the best time to start something); and horary astrology (answering a question with a chart). Some other factors taken into consideration by the ancients were fixed stars, Arabic Parts or Lots, and eclipses. In this chapter, I have chosen the subject of electional astrology—the time when something new is started. As people are totally unaware that astrology influences everything they do, projects can be started at the worst possible time—sometimes even life–threatening, as in this case. I am referring to the sinking of the Titanic.

The idea for the Titanic and her two sister ships were discussed at a meeting between The White Star Line and

Cunard in London, in July 1907. The scheme was publicly announced on 11th September 1907. (Note the date.) It must have been shortly after this that work began on the plans, but there is no available information on the exact date.

The astrological information I shall be using includes: a fixed star called Scheat (pronounced SKEET); an Arabic Part called the Part of Peril; eclipses and moon phases; the 1st, 4th, 8th and 9th houses; and an asteroid called Vesta (⚶). To explain this information, I shall first look at the fixed star 'Scheat'. It is located at 29 degrees of Pisces and is associated with extreme misfortune and drowning. It has the nature of Mercury and Mars—and should either of these planets aspect it, the star becomes more volatile.

Eclipses and Moon Phases

Eclipses and moon phases have a bearing on this tragedy. Each eclipse has a meaning of its own. When our charts are activated by eclipses, the meaning of the eclipse will come to light.

There are twelve houses in a chart, starting on the left-hand side and moving anti-clockwise. The important houses relating to the Titanic's story are the 1st, which would be represent the ship's body; the 4th house, which deals with endings; the 8th, which deals with transformation and the 9th, which relates to long-distance journeys.

As this story unfolds, I will introduce these components at the appropriate places, along with some charts. But before I begin, there are a few new factors that have come to light since January 2017.

When dealing with clients' charts, I normally introduce five asteroids. These help to define the personality more accurately. When I ran the departure chart from Southampton, I couldn't understand why Vesta (⚚) was prominently placed in the 1st house all by itself. I was soon to be enlightened. On 1st January 2017, a documentary was shown on TV revealing new evidence relating to the tragedy. What emerged was nothing short of criminal. So let's return to the beginning—and a timeline of the events leading up to her sinking.

We start on 18th January 1908. The first event was a lunar eclipse at 27 degrees of Cancer. As mentioned before, eclipses have a meaning of their own. This particular eclipse is concerned with "ending or separation, or dealing with a parting from someone travelling overseas". This eclipse was aspecting the fixed star Scheat. There was trouble with this project from the very beginning. If you take the meaning of the eclipse and add it to the meaning of the fixed star, you can see how the ending would manifest.

The next prominent date is the day the 'Titanic' was launched from Belfast: which was 31 May 1911, at 12:13 p.m. (Fig 11). At this time, Mars was at the same degree as Scheat. I mentioned earlier that any planet of the same nature as the fixed star makes the star more volatile. Mars is of the nature as Scheat. The Ascendant is Virgo, and Mercury, its ruler. is in the 8th house. along with Saturn. which rules icebergs.

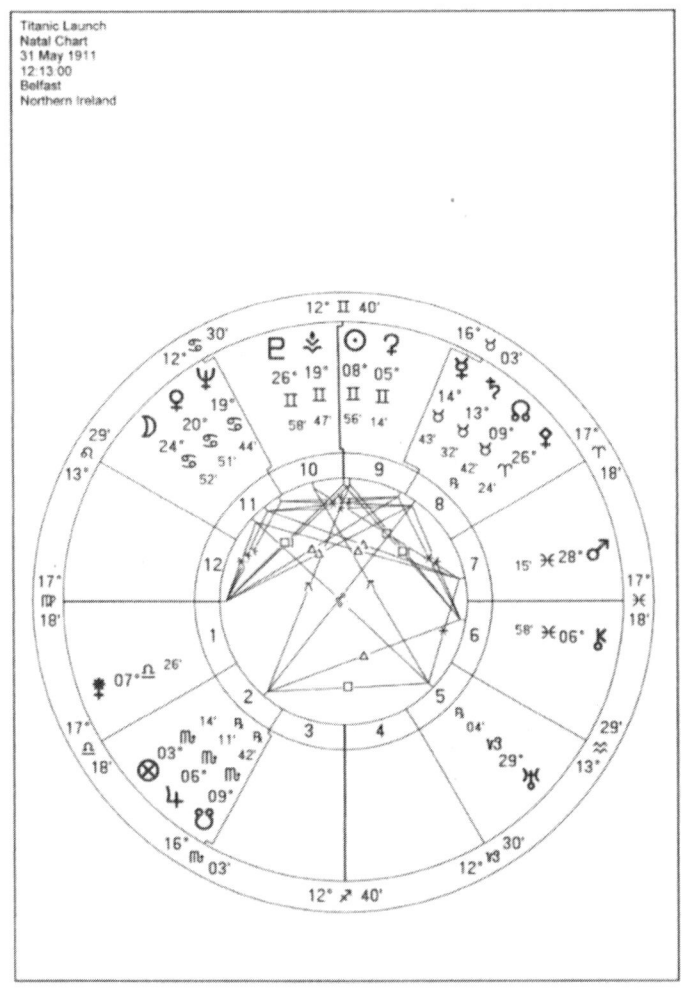

Fig 11

On 22 October 1911, there was a solar eclipse at 29 degrees of Libra, aspecting Scheat. This eclipse deals with sudden endings and traumatic transformation through news received. The aspect was at 150 degrees from Scheat, which means moving into a new situation.

Continuing with the moon phases, there was a new moon at 27 degrees of Pisces, next to Scheat, on 18 March 1912. On 2 April 1912, at 8 p.m. Titanic left Belfast for Southampton (Fig 12). The Ascendant and the Moon are close to the point where the eclipse took place on 22 October 1911. But if you look at the 10th house, you will find the asteroid Vesta (⚶)—and this is where the story, as we know it, begins to change, and the truth starts to emerge.

Vesta is a lamp, a naked flame. Placed in the 10th house, it's out in the open for all to see—but it is forming a tight 30-degree angle to Saturn. So Saturn will try to restrict something from being made public.

On 1 January 2017, a documentary was televised, bringing new evidence to light. A family, while clearing out the loft of a relative, found a photograph album with pictures of the Titanic at Southampton. She had a large black mark on her side. The pictures were taken to experts, and it was concluded that Titanic was on fire, and that she had been when she left Belfast. The crew were sworn to secrecy—hence Vesta's aspect to Saturn (♄) in the 7th house of open enemies, in the sign of Taurus, which rules the voice.

There was another picture showing three crewmen leaving the ship, and more staff had to be taken on in Southampton.

There was a frantic attempt to put the fire out. The fire had started where the coal had been loaded—it had become overheated and started to smoulder.

On 12 April 1912, at 12 noon, Titanic sailed (Fig 13). When I first saw this chart, my immediate reaction was: *What is Vesta doing there, all by itself in the 1st house?*—but this was before the TV broadcast. It all made sense then.

Vesta is in the 1st house, in Leo, a fire sign. The Ascendant, or 1st house, shows what danger, if any, the body of the ship was in.

It is at this point that the Arabic Parts, or Lots, come into play. The 1st house cusp is next to the Part of Peril. Venus, the ruler of the 4th house of endings, is at the same degree as Scheat, in the 9th house of long-distance journeys.

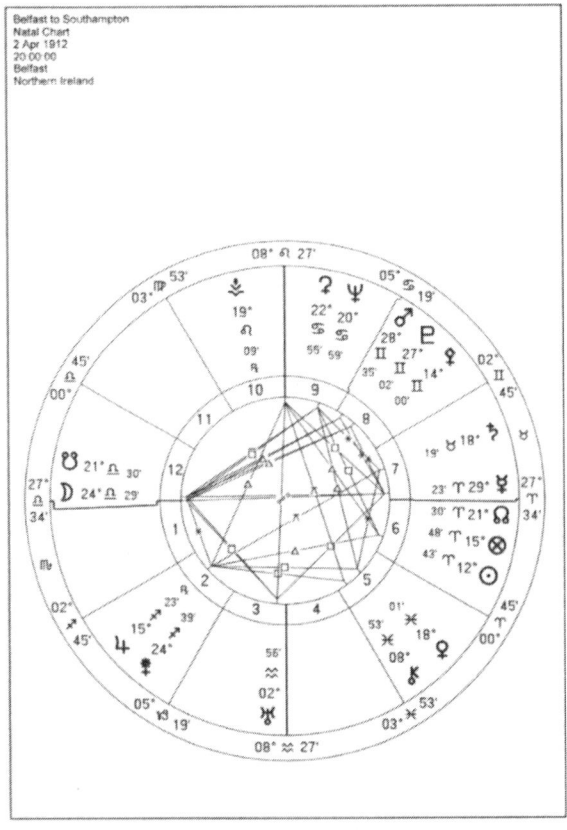

Fig 12

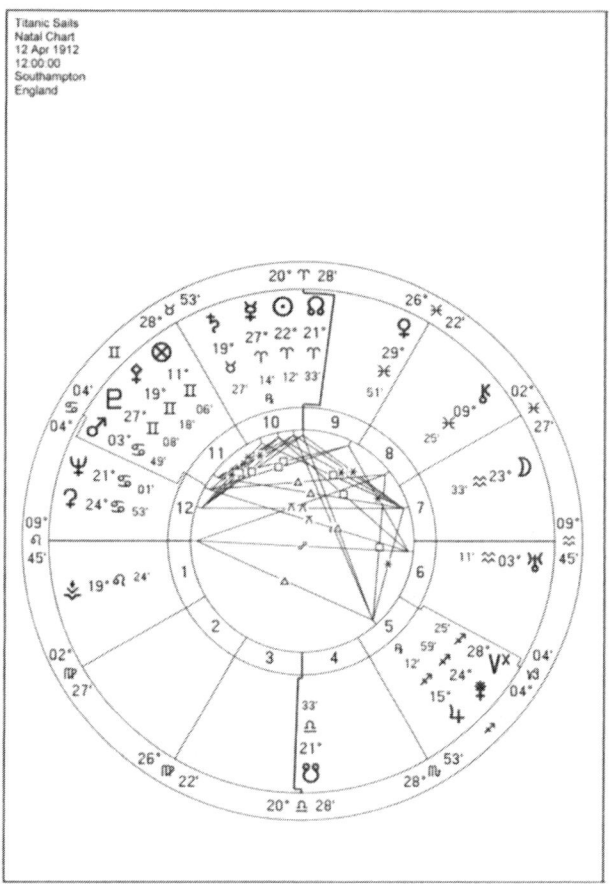

Fig 13

On 14 October 1912, at 11:40, Titanic hit the iceberg (Fig 14). More evidence came to light that she was travelling so fast she didn't have time to manoeuvre out of the way. The reason was that the men in the boiler room were continually shuffling coal into the boiler in an attempt to empty the coal storage unit, where the fire had begun.

The Moon in this chart is at 25 degrees of Pisces, aspecting Scheat. Mars, the ruler of the 4th house of endings, is very weak in the sign of Cancer, showing an ending in deep water.

On 15 April 1912, at 02:20 (Fig 15), Titanic sank. The Moon was at the same degree as Scheat.

Astrology shows what can happen if no heed is taken of what is unfolding, 1,513 souls were lost that night, and all of this was avoidable.

Between 19 April 1912 and 25 May 1912, the Americans held an enquiry into the disaster. Some of the crew who survived gave evidence relating to the fire. Between 2 May 1912 and 3 July 1912, a British Board of Enquiry was held, and more disturbing events unfolded there. The person who chaired the enquiry played down the events surrounding the fire, and it turned out he had financial interests in the White Star Line.

In July 2019, this documentary was shown again—only two weeks before I made a visit to the Titanic museum in Belfast. My main purpose was to see the photos that were found, but to my disappointment, they are not being held there.

This is a sad tale, and one that could have been avoided. We will never know if the astrologers of the day had seen what was unfolding—but if they had, would anyone connected with the ship have taken any notice?

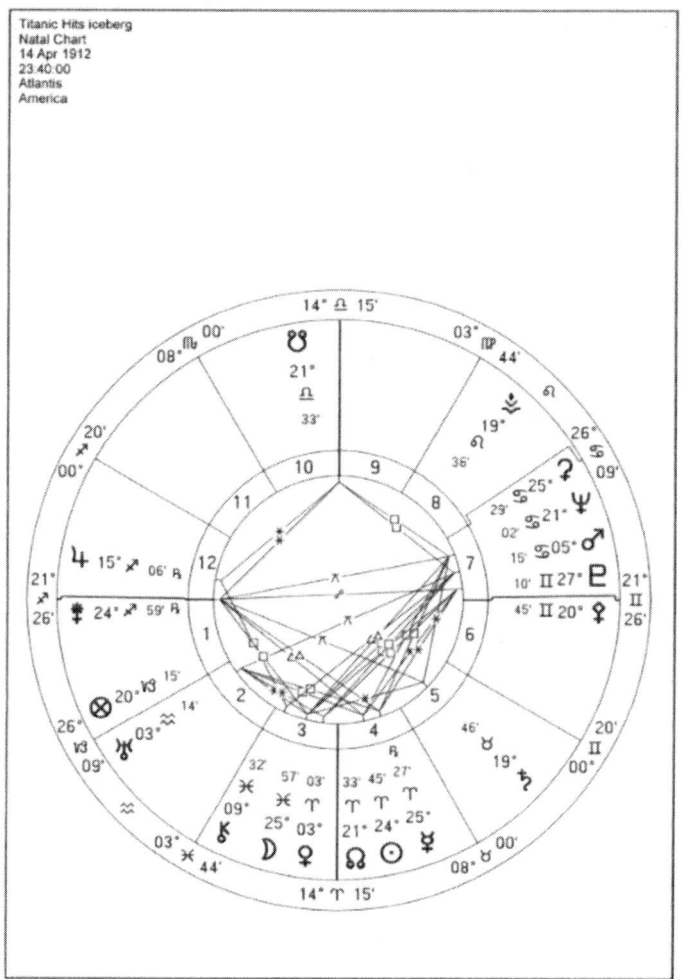

Fig 14

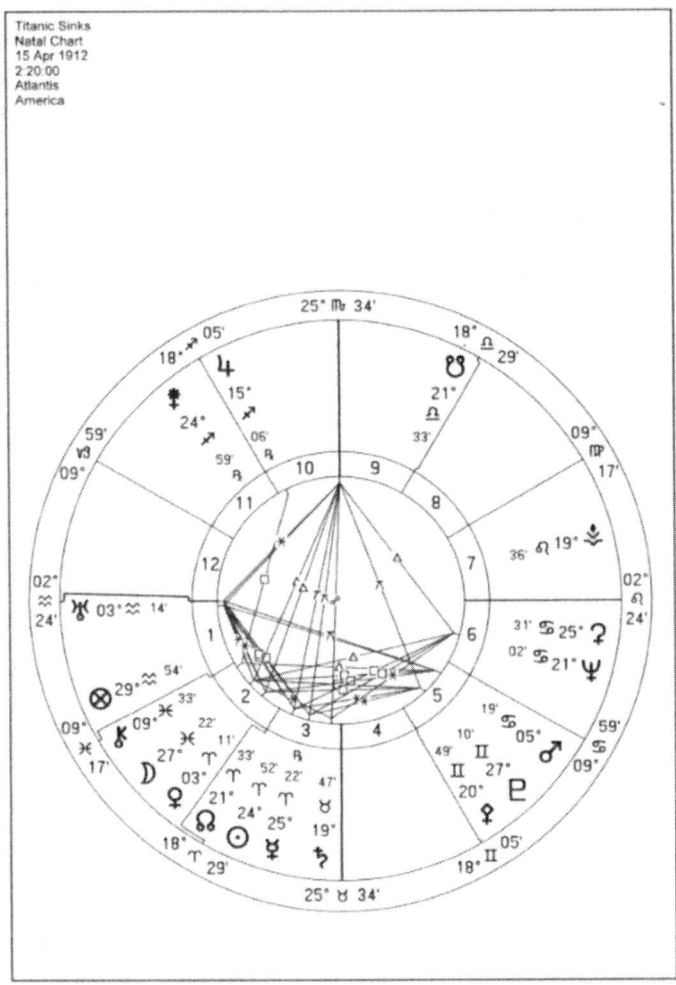

Fig 15

Chapter 11
To Close

I hope this book has helped to answer any questions on why astrology can help. Some regard this subject as entertainment, but with some of the material explained, it is anything but. I have kept the language as simple as possible—not to overload anyone with too much detail, but without leaving out anything that is important. My wish has always been to alleviate any fear—hence the importance of Chapter 2. This is a gift for us to use. Understand yourself and what you are here to do, and you will find the road of life much easier to travel. My best wishes to all who read this book.

Bibliography

The Bible (King James Version)

Predictive Astrology – Brady, Bernadette
First published as *The Eagle and the Lark*
Samuel Weiser, 1992

Christian Astrology – William Lilly
First published 1647
Astrology Classics, 2004
Astrology Centre of America

Luna Shadows III – Dietrech Pessin
Igloo Press
Tucson, Arizona

The Astrologer's Handbook
Harper Perennial

Fixed Stars & Constellations in Astrology – Robson, Vivian, B.Sc.
Astrology Centre of America

Rex Bell's Book of Rulerships
American Federation of Astrologers